Career
Shifting

Career Shifting

Starting Over in a Changing Economy

WILLIAM CHARLAND, JR.

BOB ADAMS, INC.
PUBLISHERS
Holbrook, Massachusetts

Published by Bob Adams, Inc.
260 Center Street
Holbrook, Massachusetts 02343

ISBN: 1-55850-259-9

Printed in the United States of America.

J   I   H   G   F   E   D   C   B

This publication is designed to provide accurate and authoritative information with
regard to the subject matter covered. It is sold with the understanding that the
publisher is not engaged in rendering legal, accounting, or other professional advice.
If legal advice or other expert assistance is required, the services of a competent
professional person should be sought.

— From a *Declaration of Principles* jointly adopted by a
Committee of the American Bar Association and a
Committee of Publishers and Associations

COVER DESIGN: Marshall Henrichs

This book is available at quantity discounts for bulk purchases.
For information, call 1-800-872-5627.

For Stephanie and Rachael,
Lydia and Willy Paul

Foreword

This book is the product of interviews with many people who gave generously of their time. I appreciate their contributions, and also wish to thank Phil Burgess, President of the Center for the New West, for providing a collegial setting and support services while I was writing the manuscript. Many thanks also to my wife Phoebe for her encouragement and help with text editing.

While I am grateful to all these friends and associates, it's important to note that the interpretations and conclusions drawn in this book are mine alone. *Career Shifting* is a personal vision of our options in a changing workplace.

William A. Charland, Jr.
Denver, Colorado

Contents

PART III
New Learning:
Staying Current in a Changing Economy

PART I

The Future at Work:
How the American Workplace
Is Changing

Chapter One

Shifting Gears in a Changing Workplace

Jobs can change overnight. If you've picked up this book, chances are you know that. It may be that the skills you use at work are changing. Or perhaps you've lost your job and are considering changing fields altogether. In either case, you're not alone.

Labor-market analysts estimate that each year in America one-third of our job roles are in transition, one-third of our technical skills become obsolescent, and one-third of our workers leave their jobs.

That's the challenge of a changing economy. The question is how to maintain our careers in a workplace that is constantly in transition.

Sometimes the American economy seems like a gigantic version of Asteroids—that video game where the player is a little dot in the middle of the screen and all sorts of objects come crashing in on him. The object is to zap the attacking asteroids with a laser gun, to annihilate them before they get you. But the spheroids come firing in at different angles, from every possible direction. About the time you've targeted one asteroid, another two or three are hurtling toward you.

That's what it's like trying to manage a career these days, keeping track of all the new developments in a turbulent economy. Sometimes it all becomes too much, and we'd give anything just to call time and start the game over.

Actually, you can do that in Asteroids. You can make yourself disappear from the screen and re-enter at another position. The trouble is, you can't predict where you'll reappear. It could be any place on the screen, and that could cause problems.

You'd have to learn a whole new set of reflexes, because there'll be asteroids again. That's the name of the game. So the question is whether to maintain your present position or assume the risks of a new one. It's a fundamental question, in Asteroids or in working life.

Today many Americans are at that juncture.

Not long ago I was talking with a manager in a large corporation. Several thousand managers in that company were to be let go the following year, and it was conceivable that he could be among them. Somehow we got talking about a couple who had changed careers and bought a barbecue restaurant in the mountain resort community of Steamboat Springs, Colorado. I was exclaiming about their barbecue sauce and their lifestyle in the mountains when I noticed that I seemed to have lost the corporate manager's attention. He was staring out his office window, toward the mountains.

"Herb," I said. "Are you still here?"

"I'm not sure," he answered. "You know I've been fooling with a barbecue sauce for several years. Some of my friends have told me I should market it . . . ."

That's the Asteroids dilemma.

For some time now, I've been studying the American economy while trying to help people find their place in it. I'm a specialist in employment and training. It's a calling that stems from my own career. I began as a college chaplain some thirty years ago, then became a college teacher in the South in order to take part in the civil rights movement of the 1960s. As I got a bit older, I turned to the field of adult education and became director of an innovative adult-education program, University Without Walls.

Most of my students in the UWW program were about thirty-five years old—my age at the time—and I identified with the struggles in their lives as they studied to complete their degrees. Employment was a major concern for most of them. I found myself drawn to job-related problems and became a career counselor.

Meanwhile, I pursued a lifelong interest in writing and produced several books. When my second book came out in 1986, a friend in public relations introduced me to a local newspaper editor, suggesting that I might write an article on employment to help publicize the book. I was excited about having contact with journalism, a field I'd enjoyed when I was editor of my college newspaper but had never studied formally. I wrote the article, then did others, and eventually became a columnist. That's how I gathered much of the material for this book.

These days I continue to specialize in the field of employment and training, but through three different job roles. I'm a journalist, a labor-market consultant, and a trainer who conducts seminars for dislocated workers. Perhaps that's my main claim to expertise when it comes to career shifting. I change fields several times a week!

Today, many people are finding ways to grow with the changing times—sometimes in the midst of personal challenges. One of my favorite examples is Joan Duncan, a woman in her sixties who found herself floundering a few years ago when her marriage of thirty years ended in divorce.

Duncan is a bright, capable person. In addition to raising several children, she had served for some years as mayor of the small suburb where she lived. But suddenly she was cast adrift on the job market with no apparent marketable skills. Taking stock of her situation, Duncan enrolled in some word processing classes at a community college and hired out as a temporary worker. It was a comedown from her role as mayor, working under someone else's direction instead of exercising leadership herself. But it was also a broadening experience; gradually she began to see a new career in it.

Duncan noticed that a number of women her age were flailing about in the labor market, learning office skills and looking for work as temporaries. There were more than a few older men out looking for work as well. Often the older people seemed to get lost in a marketplace crowded with younger workers. Yet she sensed that some employers preferred the maturity and work ethic of older workers.

One night this idea came to her: "What if there were a temporary employment service just for seniors? I wonder if I could make a living by providing the kind of help that I needed?"

Duncan did. She teamed with Larry Brady, an ex-stockbroker friend, to found Senior Skills, a temporary employment service for workers fifty-five and older. Today she and Brady operate a thriving business. It's demanding work, as they struggle to promote a new idea. But recently they received a national award for their efforts. And along the way, they found time to get married.

For John Hickenlooper, the transition to a new career began in his thirties. Hickenlooper was a geologist in Denver when the energy industry crashed in the late 1980s. First the industry faltered, as a few branch offices in Denver consolidated with headquarters back in Houston. Then it slid like an avalanche. Twenty thousand geologists lost their jobs in Denver in one year alone. Soon Hickenlooper found himself with nothing to show for his career but a diploma on the wall and a severance package.

Hickenlooper recognized that his graduate degree in geology was unmarketable, but he had no idea what else to do. He took a trip to San Francisco to visit his brother and clear his head. That's when he encountered his first brew pub. John had been an amateur homebrewer back in college. It was a hobby he'd enjoyed but never thought he could be paid for. But here was a new kind of business: the bar and grill with its own micro-brewery. "Hey," he thought after a few brews in San Francisco. "Why not?"

When he returned to Denver, Hickenlooper used his geological library research skills to explore the growing industry of micro-breweries. Then he enrolled in some small-business-development courses and developed a business plan. Before long, he was out raising capital for Colorado's first brew pub, the Wynkoop Brewery. ·

It wasn't easy to sell his idea. Hickenlooper approached his mother as an investor and she turned him down flat. But his former Little League baseball coach put up $10,000.

Today, Hickenlooper looks back on his venture with mixed feelings. Starting a new business has taken almost all his time. "My life the last few years hasn't been a lot of fun," he admits. But the brew pub is a success. The Wynkoop has expanded to include a jazz night club and an upscale billiards parlor. Located in a renovated warehouse in historic Lower Downtown Denver, the pub is just down the street from the site of Coors Field, the future stadium of Denver's new major league baseball team, the Colorado Rockies. It's a vibrant neighborhood, and the Wynkoop is at the center of the action.

Are those cases typical of American careers in our changing economy? Not entirely. I've appeared on panel discussions with Hickenlooper and Duncan and have heard plenty of mixed reactions from the audience. Some people are so depressed about their own careers that they're skeptical of any sort of new venture.

Recently I helped sponsor a panel discussion on opportunities for professional workers in temporary employment companies, and included Joan Duncan on the program. Some of the white-collar types in the audience noted that the kinds of jobs Duncan has for older workers don't begin to match the corporate jobs they themselves have lost. "This is not a roomful of secretaries," one fellow blustered.

I understand that frustration. Currently, most of the new jobs being created in the United States do not begin to pay as well as the one-third of corporate middle management jobs or the many high-paying manufacturing jobs we've lost during the past decade. It's clear that the U.S. has a severe employment crisis, with many families relying on two incomes to get by and droves of single-parent households falling into poverty. As former secretary of labor Ray Marshall puts it, "The only way we have been able to sustain our incomes is selling more labor." Now, he says, our problem is "there are not enough families with another wife to put into the workforce."

Others bewail the risks in starting a new business. When John Hickenlooper appeared in another panel on small business development, some people were quick to point out that the majority of new business ventures fail. Again, they got no argument from me.

But it's also clear to me that the American economy is in transition. What we see is not what we have to accept. *The promise lies in rebuilding our society as an economy of entrepreneurs.* And in that process, the people at the forefront are innovative, risk-takers such as Joan and John. They're the kinds of contemporary pioneers on whom our future depends.

What sets these people apart more than anything else is their capacity for new learning. Yet even in this they're not so different from the rest of us. We all have the capacity to move ahead in changing times if we can keep ourselves alive as learners. Skills are the bridge to America's new economy.

That's true not only for individuals but also for our entire society. Think of the statistics cited earlier in the form of a revolving door.

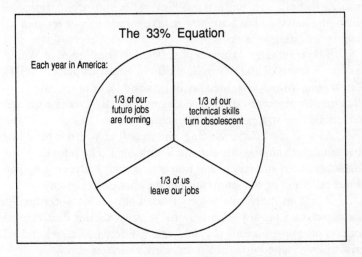

Suppose that as this chart rotated clockwise, one panel led to the next. As skills turned obsolescent, and workers left their jobs, new jobs were forming. Suppose it were possible to time that rhythm so that individuals could spot which skills were rising as others declined. They might then prepare for emerging occupations waiting in the wings.

That's not an unrealistic expectation. Many countries in Southeast Asia and Western Europe do a much better job of tracking labor market changes and re-training workers than we do in the United States. Perhaps under a new administration we'll improve our American system of workforce training. It's likely that the Clinton administration will introduce a number of innovations to help America catch up with the rest of the world's industrialized nations in job training. Already there's talk in Washington of a new Employment Insurance System that would emphasize job training rather than cash payments to the unemployed. Under one proposal for a new voucher plan, each American worker would receive a Career Opportunity Card to pay for job-related training as needed. These are exciting proposals.

But in the last analysis, maintaining a competitive workforce cannot rest on government programs. Retraining will always be a personal responsibility. It's up to each of us to maintain those skills that can keep us competitive in the changing global economy.

That is the emphasis of *Career Shifting*. This book is a consumer's guide to new learning in the changing economy. It's a resource to help you understand how skills and occupations are changing today, and to learn how to take more control over your career by updating your skills.

The book targets three topics. Part I, "The Future at Work," explores some of today's basic shifts in the workplace. Part II, "Emerging Work," is a directory of jobs and skills in specific fields that may be of interest to career changers. Part III, "New Learning," covers specific strategies for retraining.

As you read *Career Shifting*, you may find yourself browsing back and forth among the sections. That's good. The purpose of the book is to help you reflect and find connections between your personal skills and new opportunities in the changing economy.

That's an individual process that all of us must work through for ourselves. Like any other personal venture, shifting careers takes careful planning, for each person's path is different. The other day I saw this sign taped up over a postal clerk's window.

"This life is a test," it read. "It is only a test. Had this been a real life, you would have received further instructions on how to proceed and where to go."

Career Shifting is a resource for working through change in an economy that offers few printed directions but lots of options. As Joan Duncan puts it, "The first step is to recognize that the Book of Life is a loose-leaf notebook."

Chapter Two

Pyramids to Diamonds:
How the Workplace Is Changing

It's hard to make career decisions in changing times—not that it's ever been easy. Even in periods of economic stability, careers aren't static. People can outgrow their work. Elementary school teachers and pediatricians may find they're less motivated to work with small children once their own kids are grown and gone. Dancers need new careers when their legs go. Those kinds of changes are typical.

But in some eras, such as the period we're living through, everything changes at once. Not only do the needs we bring to work change, but the workplace shifts as well.

Set your sights on a job as a sushi chef, and suddenly the American taste for Japanese food sours. Learn to program in Unix and the computer industry turns to Ada. A friend of mine on the south side of Chicago used to say, "Every time I find out where it's at, somebody moves it!" She could have been describing the American economy.

That's what it's like to make plans in the midst of an economic revolution.

For that's what we're living through today. Whatever people say about an economic recession—as in "When do you think the recession will lift?"—what we really have in this country is a radical revision of the way we're doing business. It's a change in the rules of the game, not unlike the day in 1823 when a student at the English boarding school of Rugby lost his head in the middle of a soccer match. Instead of kicking the ball, he picked it up and ran with it. Everyone else had such a good time chasing him down and tackling him that they invented the sport of rugby. Like today's economic change, that was a revolution.

It's hard to measure progress in a revolution. Ralph Whitehead, a journalism professor who has studied the labor market for twenty years, compares working in the U.S. economy to standing in a dark room, knee-deep in water. Outside the room, there are voices.

"Run!" someone cries. "It's a flood."

"Now, lie down. It's a bath," says another.

These are puzzling times.

As I've studied the changing economy for a number of years—analyzing data, interviewing employers, and helping people re-arrange their careers—I've learned to look for patterns in our personal lives as well as the whole society. It's my way of measuring change. For some time now, I've been aware of three pronounced trends that seem to be affecting most people's working lives:

+ the shift from pyramid to diamond-like organizations

+ from specialized careers to new jobs for generalists

+ with new support systems in reorganized labor.

I first recognized the diamond-shaped organization when I was conducting a study of employment trends in Colorado a few years ago. I'd developed a questionnaire to find out the principal kinds of jobs found in key industries within our state. As I interviewed employers in these fields—everyone from hospital directors to hotel managers—I asked about the levels of workers they employed. How many were full-time executives and managers? How many were directly involved in producing goods or delivering a service? How many were in clerical or custodial jobs?

The pattern emerged slowly, but it was clear. In most organizations, the great majority of jobs were in the second category; most employees were producers of goods or services. They were customer-service representatives, for example, or consulting engineers. They were not full-time managers—vice presidents of this or that. Most of the organizations I surveyed had cut management staff to the bone. Not many people were paid just to supervise the work of someone else.

Nor were there many support-staff jobs at the low end of the scale. Some companies, in fact, employed no clerical support staff at all. A regional airline I know of has *no secretaries* to type and take dictation. Everyone in the organization is required to use word processing for his or her correspondence, spreadsheet software for budgeting, and so on. I'm told the same is true of a computer manufacturer in Texas: no secretaries.

I began to see that these new organizations were shaped like diamonds. They were thick in the middle with service providers and other workers who produced revenue while supervising themselves, and thin at the bottom and the top.

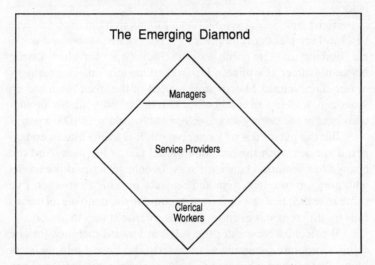

The Emerging Diamond

Managers

Service Providers

Clerical Workers

What did this pattern mean?

Well, it certainly seemed different from most of the organizations I'd grown up with. Twenty or thirty years ago, most major companies were shaped like pyramids, not diamonds. They were thick at the bottom and narrow at the top.

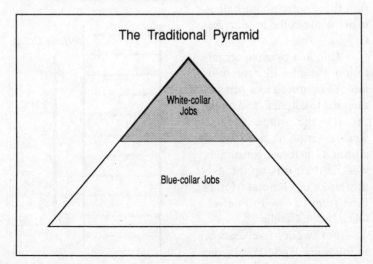

The Traditional Pyramid

White-collar Jobs

Blue-collar Jobs

Those were organizations that people could enter through low-level jobs with minimal skills, then work their way up. Some rose to middle-management positions, and a few climbed all the way to the top. Careers were based on the familiar blue-collar-to-white-collar ladder.

To be sure, such pyramid organizations aren't extinct. In Denver, I still see plenty of companies with corporate ladders, and workers climbing up. The publisher of the newspaper for which I write began his career as a printer. He worked his way up. The manager of our elite Neiman Marcus store started in the stock room eleven years ago, working after school for five dollars an hour. Six promotions later, at age twenty-seven, he's probably making $60,000 a year.

But the pyramid is no longer typical. It is fading like an endangered species, with the diamond model taking its place. And the change has profound consequences. In counseling mid-life adults who grew up in one system and now are working in another, I've come to realize that the shift from pyramid to diamond organizations calls for different values and strategies when it comes to careers.

We need to reconsider the value of upward mobility, for one thing. Corporate pyramids were tiered. The lowest jobs were for blue-collar workers who were directly involved in production. They made things with their hands. To progress in a pyramid, one worked up into the ranks of white-collar positions. Those were the jobs for supervisors and managers who no longer had to work with their hands but supervised others who did. In a typical corporation there were about half as many white-collar as blue-collar jobs.

Life in a pyramid organization was a lot like the military. You entered as a private, then made corporal, and on up through the rungs. Careers were a series of steps to be climbed, just as consumers worked their way up through the ranks of General Motors cars: from Chevy to Pontiac, Olds, Buick, Cadillac.

For twenty-five years or so following World War II, the

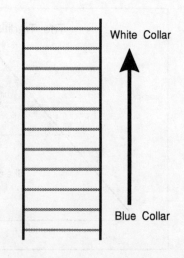

The Ladder in Our Minds

White Collar

Blue Collar

American corporate economy, with its stratified organizations, was very successful. This period—from 1945 to about 1970—marked the greatest economic expansion in the history of the world. America, as the sole surviving industrial power, led the way.

Like any powerful institution, the corporate pyramid made a deep impression on the values of our entire society. That's why most people who grew up in the corporate era still value upward mobility at a gut level and secretly hope to find themselves climbing up some sort of ladder in their careers.

Every week or so I run into an ex-corporate employee who's now working as an independent consultant, with a business card that identifies him as Joe Schmo: President of Joe Schmo Associates (his dog and his cat). Sometimes he's also listed as the CEO. That's the power of the ladder in our minds.

The other relic of the old corporate ladder is the aversion many Americans have for manual work. They're drawn to white-collar professions where people work with their heads, not their hands. But those professions, like jobs for corporate middle managers and chief executive officers, are crumbling like the pyramids. Today there are fewer and fewer traditional white-collar jobs around.

Consider a few examples.

Law. A 1991 article in the *Washington Post* reported that 44 percent of the nation's 250 largest law firms had cut staff during the previous year. The pattern prevailed across the United States in every major city except (you guessed it) Washington, D.C.

Architecture. An estimated 25 percent of architects in several major American cities—principally on the East Coast—are unemployed.

Similar figures apply to *public relations*: 25 percent unemployment, nationwide. The same pattern can be found in other white-collar business specialties, such as strategic planning.

Yet, despite the scarcity of corporate jobs, we continue to spawn white-collar specialists. Law school enrollment is at an all-time high (129,580 at last count) and MBAs are multiplying like rabbits. That's not to say that the education these people have received is without value. Most specialized academic fields are personally enriching: it's stimulating to be able to think like a lawyer, conceive designs as an architect, or plan a media campaign as a public-relations specialist might do.

The problem is finding work in white-collar professions. Many highly-trained professionals have relied upon large corporate employers to employ them in specialized niches such as managerial development or strategic planning. But today the corporate economy is fading. Analysts estimate that America has lost one million corporate white-collar jobs a year recently, and that one-third of all middle management jobs are history.

That's why it's time to re-set our sights when it comes to career-planning. The day of the protective corporate employer is past. We're living in a time when jobs are joint ventures, employers are partners, and careers are continuing education. It's a day of transition and a time for new learning.

Chapter Three

New Jobs for Generalists

M eanwhile, for those who can look beyond the traditional corporate pyramid and the ladder in our heads, there are some exciting new developments in diamond organizations. A whole array of new jobs are appearing that are neither white collar nor blue collar, but something in between. They're new jobs for generalists.

In part II of this book, "Emerging Work," I'll profile a number of these new occupations in a variety of fields. But first I want to describe some patterns to look for in the jobs, to suggest how they're developing throughout our economy.

The new jobs have several important characteristics. Most of them are in smaller organizations, where most of America's new employment growth is to be found. They're usually for front-line production workers and others who work directly with customers—not for full-time managers.

They're also multi-problem positions. Career writer Tom Jackson once observed, "A job is a problem to be solved." That's always been the case. But these days, most new jobs address more than one problem. That's why they often call for new and sometimes unconventional combinations of skills.

Here's an example of the old jobs and the new in telecommunications. US WEST, a regional phone company, is an enormous corporation with fifty thousand employees in fourteen states, many of these employees occupying highly specialized roles. But the organization is downsizing, and many specialized jobs are being discontinued.

I've worked with US WEST employees who are seeking new jobs with resumes based on what they did in the old corporate pyramid. The resumes are filled with acronyms such as LAPGAP and SLAP. That's "Local and Pair Gain Analysis Program" and "Specific Loop Analysis Program," for the uninitiated.

In trying to help these over-specialized workers, I show them how to develop resumes that describe their skills in broad, functional terms. LAPGAP and SLAP, for example, are "computer-based programs for cost management and pricing." That's still a narrow niche, but it connects to other industries where the same kind of work may go on. Translating trade talk is one way to help overcome the problem of over-specialization.

But there are even greater differences between corporate pyramids and diamond-shaped organizations, old jobs and new. In today's flatter, more flexible firms, workers not only need broader skills, they also need to work more independently.

Take the cellular telephone industry. In the fast-changing world of telecommunications, cellular phone companies have been growing at a record clip even as large corporations such as US WEST are downsizing. One cellular company I know virtually doubled its staff in a year, from 85 employees to 170. But the kinds of people they're hiring are very different from the LAPGAP and SLAP specialists. Cellular sales representatives in particular need skills such as analyzing business communication needs, credit reports, and financing arrangements, as well as cellular technology. They're required to handle the full sales cycle with very little support—understanding customers' needs, product lines, and financing options, and even processing credit applications (a process that takes only twenty minutes).

Cellular phones are typical of today's volatile high-tech industries, where product lives are short (the modern cellular industry itself is only ten years old) and technology must be tied to customers' needs. Cellular sales reps need to be non-stop learners. That's why the personnel manager for one company carries the title, "Director of People Development." It's an apt title for an environment where skills and jobs are constantly evolving.

In small organizations, jobs may change too fast for written descriptions. To understand them, we need to grasp the needs they are intended to fill. Here are two typical examples.

Jeff Ransom owns the best graphic-arts company in his city. He started the business eight years ago with a single employee. Today his firm has a staff of twenty and a half-million-dollar annual budget. Jeff knows every facet of the graphic-arts business; he learned it from the ground up.

But nothing had prepared him for desktop publishing. The new technology first surfaced several years ago. Jeff noticed an ad in a graphic design publication, then sat in on a demonstration at a trade show.

He dismissed it quickly. Desktop publishing programs couldn't begin to compare with the work his graphic artists and camera specialists did. Jeff concentrated his efforts on top-quality graphics and hired the best artists he could find.

But desktop publishing wouldn't go away. More and more companies acquired publishing software that ran on their micro computers, then invested in laser-jet printers. The quality of in-house publishing improved every year.

Last year Jeff's business began to decline. Now he faces the prospect of laying off the same artists he worked hard to recruit. He's thought of offering some public seminars on how to combine graphic arts with desktop publishing. The seminars might bring in additional revenue and sales leads, while establishing a new role for his company. But who could lead the seminars and market them? Could any of his artists be trained to do that?

Laurel Olson owns a complex of apartment buildings. She and her late husband, Eric, built the apartments fifteen years ago with a government loan. The buildings were designed with senior citizens in mind.

Eric Olson was a contractor with a good business sense. He recognized that the numbers of seniors were growing in his city. And he saw there were federal funds available to subsidize their housing. But now Eric is gone, and Laurel Olson is concerned about the apartments. Many of the elderly residents who moved in fifteen years ago are still there. Like most older people, they're living longer—"aging in place." But some are having difficulty caring for themselves. And federal guidelines require that senior citizens in subsidized housing maintain an independent lifestyle.

Last month an inspector came by and transferred four of the residents to nursing homes. Laurel suffered a financial loss. But it also bothered her to see people she'd come to know and care about carted off to an institution. In a couple of instances, she felt the residents might have been able to maintain their independence and keep their apartments with the help of just one or two special services, such as shopping.

Laurel has begun to re-evaluate her staffing needs for the apartment complex. Gus, the building manager, does a fine job of keeping up the place. But he's no social worker; he wasn't hired for that. Maybe there's a need for another, new kind of employee. Is there such a thing as a social worker who can do maintenance?

How would you have filled those two jobs? What kind of applicants would you have looked for? When I use these examples in workshops, I generally divide the audience into discussion groups and introduce them to this grid.

	NEED	SKILL	OCCUPATION
EMERGING			
ONGOING			
DECLINING			

As you see, the chart has three vertical columns and three lateral columns. The labels on the side represent three levels of market demand: declining, ongoing, and emerging. At the top are three components of working life: need, skill, and occupation. I ask everyone to approach these cases on the top line from left to right. What need(s) is emerging in each situation? What skill(s) is required to meet the need? And what job title might we give a person who used the skill to meet the need?

Jeff Ransom's case illustrates a widespread, mounting need for people who can understand new technology, apply it to a particular task or profession, and help others learn to use it. We might call that occupation "technical trainer." But it's not clear that the person Jeff hires will come from the training profession. He'll probably look for artists on his staff who have a bent toward teaching and marketing rather than hire a professional trainer and try to teach that person what the artists know.

The case raises an important point when it comes to emerging work. Needs give rise to skills, but they don't always create full-blown occupations. Often the skills are added to existing jobs.

In Laurel Olson's case, the skills needed cover a broad range of abilities: from building maintenance to social work. It's a reminder of the many instances today in which "blue-collar" manual skills and "white-collar" intellectual and interpersonal skills are parts of the same job. (Think of how difficult it is to classify either Jeff's job or Laurel's as a blue- or white-collar occupation.)

What would you call Laurel's job? In a workshop the other day, someone came up with the title "geriatric concierge." Maybe that's as good as any. For more about this occupation, see "Access Coordinators for the Elderly" in chapter 14, "Residential Management."

I use the entire grid when I'm counseling mid-career workers, to help them consider the various components of their careers. Which needs, skills, and occupations in their careers are emerging, ongoing, or declining? One of the worst mistakes in a changing economy is to assume that if one's occupation declines, all of one's skills go down the tubes with it.

That's not true. Consider the case of uranium geologists. That was a thriving field until the accident at Three Mile Island. Soon afterward, uranium geology in America collapsed like a house of cards. The only apparent market for the skills of uranium geologists was in South Africa, where most of them did not care to live.

But as the ecological crisis deepened and the environmental management industry arose, it turned out that many geologists had solid skills that could be transferred into the new field. It was not so much their education in earth science but their experience in project management that counted. The same skills geologists had used in managing exploration projects out in the wilderness were vital to environmental cleanup. Those skills had a life of their own.

Of course, it's equally true that new skills don't always create new occupations. Sometimes new skills like desktop publishing mesh with old professions like graphic arts because that's the most efficient way to meet a particular set of needs. Word processing is another example of a skill that's been added to existing jobs. Today there are many more professionals who use word processing to write their own correspondence than there are full-time word processors.

   That's why it's difficult for anyone to predict the future of an occupation. And that's why it's important, in managing our careers and planning courses of training, to concentrate on the skills required to meet important needs and let occupations take care of themselves.

   If the market is there, one can practice a skill as a specialist. If there's no need for specialists but the skill still has value, there'll be a place for generalists. In a day when jobs come and go, skills are the place to focus our energies. They're our best bridge to jobs in the new economy.

Chapter Four

Strategies for Staying Current

A book is a conversation.
"All right,," you may be saying about now. "I get the picture. Specialists are out, generalists are in. The message is, Broaden your skills.

"But how? I've been plucking turkeys so long, it's spoiled me for anything else. All I know is my specialized skills. How do I go about becoming more of a generalist?"

It's a good question, for learning new skills is always easier said than done—especially when we're busy working. I remember calling on a fellow worker first thing one morning and finding her hunched over a packing crate in the middle of her office. It had arrived overnight. In the carton was a computer that Sarah's boss had seen at a trade show. He'd liked the machine so well that he'd scrounged up some funds and ordered one for every member of his staff.

Sarah liked the looks of the computer, too. But she had a deskful of work, and no idea when she'd find time to learn how to operate it. So there she stood—immobilized—staring at the container in the middle of the floor.

Today one of the major employee benefits of many jobs is the quality of learning they provide. Companies such as Xerox, Kodak, and Motorola are known as much for their educational environments as for their salaries or health benefits. By the same token, other organizations that enter new fields or introduce technology without training are infamous for their inefficiency and for the stress they cause employees. Just ask Sarah.

Many analysts suggest that's a key factor in career planning. If we can find a job in a leading-edge company and participate in their in-house training program, then most of our career development needs will take care of themselves.

Some say we should hire on with a learning-rich organization even if the available jobs don't match our interests. The point is to get in the system, qualify for in-house training, and learn which skills the organization considers important to the kind of job we do want. Then, after acquiring those skills, we can apply for a transfer.

I've seen people use that strategy to enter the growing field of health care. They trade on computer skills, for example, to get a job in a hospital, then take in-house training courses to qualify for a job in patient care. Not only do they receive tuition benefits from their employer, but they learn which skills have market value—based on the training their employer is willing to pay for. In addition, it's usually easier to get hired in a new job if one is transferring from another part of the industry. It's hard to change what we do and where we work all at the same time.

Hospitals are a hotbed of new learning. Recently I interviewed the chief administrator in a hospital that belongs to a large, multinational health care corporation. The corporation prides itself on staying at the forefront of new technology, both for the benefit of patients and also to control costs.

The pace of change in medicine is phenomenal. Last year, this hospital introduced fifteen new treatment technologies. Each technique required a new set of skills. Because procedures are changing so fast, the hospital is doing almost all of its training in-house. "Schools can't keep up with us," the administrator said. "Our industry won't stand still long enough to set up degree programs in new technology."

He described a new technique for testing the elasticity of a patient's spine prior to surgery. It's one of those new methods, like magnetic resonance imaging, that reduces unwarranted surgery and increases the efficiency of operations. The hospital had trained two employees to run the testing program, and it seemed both were doing well. Each was earning about $35,000 a year. But there the similarity ended. One of the technicians making $35,000 had a high school diploma, and the other had a PhD! It was skills, not degrees, that had value.

That's the benefit of finding a workplace where we can stay current. For many of us, it's what we learn—not what we earn—that matters most in the long run.

One of the best on-the-job learning environments I've seen is Stapleton Airport, the Denver facility that's infamous for shutting down during snowstorms—which is a major reason it's about to be replaced by a new airport with more runways on the outskirts of town. The new Denver International Airport will feature state-of-the-art technology in every facet of its operations. Meanwhile, Stapleton is serving as the test site and training ground for the new technology. The old airport is one of those rare public facilities that consistently turns a profit, and for some years civic officials have plowed their surplus revenues into all sorts of new equipment. Airlines have followed suit.

Not long ago I visited the baggage-handling operation of one of the airlines. Two tiers below ground level, I found a beehive of activity in a big cavernous space that looked like a set from a James Bond movie. Dozens of workers in blue uniforms were processing thirteen thousand pieces of luggage a day—twenty-nine thousand during ski season. They were using all kinds of technology—from computers to laser scanners to voice-recognition devices.

One employee was steering baggage by the sound of his voice. When he muttered "Atlanta," a suitcase scooted off to the right. "Detroit," and the next bag headed left. In addition to all the high-tech equipment, there were motorized carts hauling baggage and even a couple of people on bicycles who picked up strays that had slipped through the cracks of the system.

The baggage manager told me that it's impossible to find technicians who can work with all those kinds of equipment, so he hires people who are trained in one of the craft trades—electrical or mechanical systems or electronics—and helps them learn the rest. The educational process extends to baggage handlers, who are trained to enter and retrieve data from computers. "Even the guy in knee pads, throwing bags against the bulkheads, he's getting data off a computer screen," he told me.

That's the kind of workplace more of us will learn to look for as the economy continues to generate new skills: a place where the job description includes new learning. Sometimes those learning environments will be in bright, shiny corporations and high-tech hospitals. Other times they'll be behind the scenes in hidden chambers like the subterranean baggage-handling operations at Stapleton Airport. It's another reason for being open to all sorts of occupations, not just traditional white-collar roles.

Shoshana Zuboff, a Harvard industrial psychologist who wrote the classic study of computers in the workplace, *In the Age of the Smart Machine*, found that the best learning environment in many companies was on the night shift. That's where workers had time to tinker with new technology.

For those who are independently employed, there are other

first-rate learning resources available in a cluster of organizations I call "reorganized labor." These groups, which are described in more detail in part II, mushroomed in the past decade. That's because the number of business enterprises in the United States grew $5\frac{1}{2}$ times faster than the population during the 1980s.

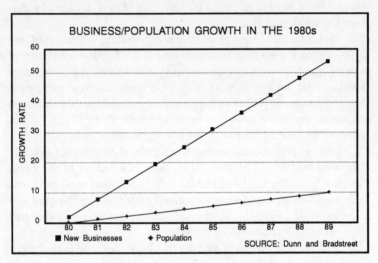

Many of the people who became entrepreneurs during the eighties did so by default. They were white-collar specialists thrust into a world of generalists, and they lacked business skills. Ex-corporate managers may have been taught how to prepare a budget plan, but they had no idea how to write a business plan that included market analysis as well as finances. Yet that was the kind of information that lending institutions required.

It was these reluctant entrepreneurs who turned for help to *small-business incubators, franchising organizations, temporary-employment services, and professional associations.* All of these institutions, with the exception of the incubators, had existed prior to 1980. But the flood of new business owners that accompanied corporate downsizing caused each of them to grow much faster than they ever had before. *They all grew at an average of 10 percent a year.* Their growth is even more dramatic when compared to the decline of corporate employment.

While many factors contributed to the growth of reorganized labor—professional associations do political lobbying, for example— the bottom-line benefit in most of these organizations is education. Franchisors, small-business incubators, and professional associations

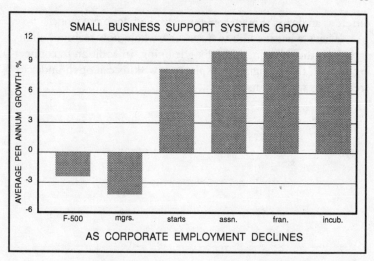

SMALL BUSINESS SUPPORT SYSTEMS GROW

AS CORPORATE EMPLOYMENT DECLINES

are essentially learning organizations. Temporary-employment services are rapidly taking on the same function. Reorganized labor is a support system for lifelong learning.

That's a very promising development, not just for our economic life but for our lives as individuals. For all of us have untapped abilities that we may never discover unless we're challenged to develop new skills in our work.

The other day I met Mel Meyer, a Catholic Marianist Brother who is also an exceptional artist. Meyer's sculptures and paintings are shown all over the world. The Adam's Mark Hotel across from Royals' Stadium in Kansas City, Missouri, is a veritable gallery of his work. Every year thousands of people visit the Marianist Gallery on the campus of a Catholic high school in Kirkwood, Missouri, a suburb of St. Louis, to see the latest phase in his growth as an artist. Meyer's giant abstract paintings exude a powerful spiritual vitality and streaming color.

Yet when Meyer graduated from college thirty years ago, he had never studied art. He was trained as a high-school English and social studies teacher. In his second year of teaching, the school where he'd been assigned lost its art instructor. Somebody had to fill the void and Meyer was asked if he'd enroll in an art education class or two. He did, and that's how he stumbled upon his talent.

Today, despite his fame, he still approaches art like a schoolchild at recess. When I met him in the gallery, he was peering at one of his most recent works—a great red and purple abstract painting—with a kind of wonder. He walked all around and examined it from different angles as though someone else had done the work.

That's what it's like to discover a whole new realm of ability, and that's the meaning of lifelong learning. In addition to connecting us with the changing workplace, new skills can open undiscovered places within ourselves.

Chapter Five

Expanding Skills

Sometimes it seems to me that one of the most powerful forces behind today's new economy has nothing to do with the economy at all. It may be that the reason American corporations are being recast from pyramids to diamonds is not just economic efficiency but because of our desire for more diversified, challenging jobs. Ask entrepreneurs what excites them about owning a business and you're apt to hear it's the opportunity to learn new skills.

I think most of us would rather have a broad job in a small organization than be stuck like a brick in someone else's pyramid. We'd prefer a job that's too broad to one that's too narrow. Most of us are stimulated by the chance to learn new skills.

A few years ago, David Kolb, a social psychologist who heads the department of organizational behavior at Case Western Reserve University, conducted a study of two very different groups of alumni: engineering graduates and social work graduates. He measured the kinds of skills people in each group had acquired in their initial training, plus the additional skills they'd found it necessary to learn in mid-career.

In some ways, the two groups were mirror images of one another. Whereas engineers had been highly trained in technical subjects, as time went on those who became managers found it necessary to learn more "soft" skills, such as psychology.

For the social workers, the pattern was just the opposite. They'd learned to work with people at the outset. But by mid-career, those who became managers found they needed more "hard" skills in budget management, computer operations, and the like.

When Kolb asked the engineers and social workers how they felt about learning radically different skills, it turned out that most of them enjoyed it. Some said they probably would have looked for an excuse to branch out in new areas even if their jobs had not required them to do so.

That same excitement over learning turns up in one field after another, again and again. It's a major theme in the lives of many people who are creating new jobs and industries in the changing economy. Part II, "Emerging Work," is a collection of their stories, together with descriptions of the fields in which they're working. I've added a list of readings, professional associations, and other resources at the end of each section for those who would like to delve into specific fields.

Most of the material in this section has come from researching my newspaper column, "Skills Update." The column appears weekly in the *Rocky Mountain News*, a Denver daily newspaper, and is carried to other papers around the country on the Scripps Howard news wire. I enjoy writing my column. Employment is an important part of our life in the United States, and Colorado offers an interesting laboratory for the new economy. It's a relatively small and young state where there's an urgent need to develop new sources of employment. The old mainstay industries of ranching, farming, energy, lumbering, and mining are fading fast. As futurist John Naisbitt observes, "It's hard to make a living today from anything that comes out of the ground."

A couple of other observations on this region:

The West has never been extensively involved with heavy manufacturing, owing to a scarcity of water, so we've not been burdened with many plant closings. It's a case of not missing what you never had. That's why western states have been able to focus on cultivating new information industries. They're vital to the new economy, they don't require much water, and they can take root almost anywhere at all. Naisbitt, for example, conducts his trend analysis business by computer modem and FAX machine from a gorgeous mountain town that's hundreds of miles away from any big city.

The West is full of free spirits like him, and so is the new economy. My colleague, Phil Burgess, calls them Lone Eagles. They're latter-day pioneers who are forging new paths for the rest of us. Not all of these people have high-tech skills, but they're all good generalists.

I met Jim Hook as he was giving a slide show on the culture and geography of Bluff, Utah, in the motel he and his wife own there. It's the only motel I've ever seen with an auditorium. Hook and his wife bought the Recapture Lodge in 1991. It's a rustic, homey place on the main street of Bluff—an old Mormon settlement near a Navajo reservation, at the edge of the beautiful Monument Valley.

I was driving from Denver down to Phoenix when I came upon Bluff at sunset. It was a spectacular sight; the bluffs for which the town is named were glowing like embers. I decided to spend the night there, if only to catch the sunrise. As it turned out, the town offered other attractions.

"There's a Navajo restaurant down the street you might want to try," the desk clerk suggested. "Ever have beef stew and fry bread? Then, tonight, Jim Hook's showing slides to the Elderhostel class. There's a bunch of 'em down from Moab. He does a real nice job. You're welcome to join us."

At eight o'clock, after a filling meal of Navajo beef stew and fry bread, I wandered down to the auditorium and flopped in an easy chair. A dozen Elderhostel people sat around on sofas, along with a few other guests who'd found their way in from the highway.

Hook was a tall, rangy fellow, about thirty-five years of age. He told us that he and his wife were ranchers from northern Colorado who had bought the Recapture Lodge in order to raise their kids in a small town and live near the Monument Valley.

The slide show was a mixture of geological data, Indian lore, Mormon history, animal husbandry, and botany—a kind of local cultural stew. None of the information was anything I'd have gone out of my way to learn, but he presented it all with such obvious enthusiasm that it was hard not to respond to his interests. He even read selections from a book of cowboy poems.

It was about 8:30, as Hook was lecturing on the merits of raising llamas, when we heard a sudden screech of tires in the parking lot, a rush of voices, and pounding on the door.

"He's after me!" a woman screamed. She ran into the lodge.

A man in a red baseball cap emerged from the darkness, following her.

Hook excused himself, and ambled to the door. "Settle down," he told the man in the baseball cap, not unkindly.

"I'm okay, I'm okay. I'm not excited!" the fellow wheezed. "She's the one that's excited. I just come after my wife."

"Not excited?" Hook took the man's left hand and laid it on his chest. "Just feel that heart pound. Now, you take a good deep breath and relax. Settle down."

The man in the baseball cap stood still for a moment. Then he turned and walked back out to the parking lot. The desk clerk went out to talk with him. Hook's wife appeared and took the woman back to the kitchen.

Hook resumed his slide show exactly where he'd left off, and in a few minutes the woman from the parking lot joined us. We considered the advantages of raising llamas versus sheep in southern Utah. I listened with half an ear. The guy in the baseball cap was still rustling around outside. I wondered if he'd come charging back through the door, and whether someone had called the police.

But as we continued our lesson on llamas, I began to sense that no one had. I realized that we were hundreds of miles from the kinds of services people counted on in the city. Out here, there were no specialists in animal husbandry, geology, cowboy poetry, or the management of domestic violence. But there were some first-rate generalists, if you could judge by Jim Hook.

Is Hook an exceptional person? To a city-dweller in the wilds of southern Utah, he seemed so at the time. But actually, if you stop to think about the history of the United States, he's not so unusual. This country was settled by self-reliant generalists such as Hook. Those pioneers and immigrants were our forebears; they were your ancestors and mine.

Of course, most of us have grown up under different circumstances. We've been rewarded for earning advanced degrees and developing narrow skills. We're specialists. But today, as the corporate economy declines, many of us are learning to be generalists once again.

The new economy is filled with people who are doing exciting things in the midst of that transition. In "Emerging Work," we'll hear some their stories and consider some of the fresh ideas they have to offer.

Part II

Emerging Work: Scenes from the New Economy

A Note on the Chapters in This Section

How is the new workplace taking shape? What new jobs are emerging and what skills do they require? Where are the best places to look for training?

In this section we'll visit a dozen different fields to explore those questions. I've chosen these fields as I've made the rounds of many workplaces, consulting and gathering material for my newspaper columns. They illustrate the kinds of changes that are occurring in other industries as well.

The fields are listed alphabetically, with lists of resources at the end of each chapter. I recommend roaming around in this material: following leads for additional information when you find an area of interest, and skimming on to the next section when you don't.

Chapter Six

Alternative Dispute Resolution

As with many other white-collar occupations, law is beginning to feel the effects of a changing economy in a society with new kinds of needs. The problems confronting the profession range from an oversupply of attorneys to clogged courtrooms that can't keep up with the mounting flow of litigation.

While many attorneys are leaving the field and exploring new careers, others are finding some innovative ways to reform it. This chapter describes several innovations in the process of resolving disputes: arbitration, mediation, negotiation, and preventive law.

> *If the laws could speak for themselves, they would*
> *complain of the lawyers in the first place.*
> — LORD HALIFAX, 1633-1695

✦   ✦   ✦

Was there ever a time when people didn't grouse about lawyers? Lord Halifax's seventeenth-century complaints sound similar to Vice President Dan Quayle's 1991 speech before the American Bar Association. "Does America really need 70 percent of the world's lawyers?" he asked rhetorically. "Is it healthy for our economy to have 18 million new lawsuits coursing through the system annually? Is it right that people with disputes come up against staggering expense and delay?"

Alternative Law

Those were the sorts of questions Denver lawyer Curtis Shortridge found himself asking a few years ago. Ten years into the practice of law, Shortridge was becoming progressively more discouraged. Part of his frustration was playing the adversarial role of an attorney in litigation. It's a common complaint among lawyers. They get tired of playing "hired gun"—intervening in conflicts between people who have stopped talking. Lawyers get battle fatigue.

But Shortridge had an additional problem. He had lost faith in the judicial system. The state courts were overloaded. Civil suits took an average of one and a half to three years before coming to trial, and most clients couldn't afford those kinds of delays.

In 1988, Shortridge saw a solution to his dilemma. The Colorado legislature voted to establish a system of mandatory arbitration for civil cases involving damages of $50,000 or less. Shortridge, with his wife and a psychotherapist friend, founded Arbitration Mediation Associates.

It was an idealistic venture, from the services offered, to the fees they charged, to the details of interior design. In place of a typically intimidating attorney's office, with black leather chairs and shelves full of law books, AMA worked out of a small hearing room. The room was intimate, with soft gray walls, indirect lighting, and Southwestern art. In the middle was a three-sided table where two disputants and an arbitrator could communicate face-to-face.

Communication was their first objective. As Curtis Shortridge's wife Pat put it, "People want to be heard and validated by someone they trust. When we have a dispute, we want to be certain we're heard."

Alternative dispute resolution (ADR), as it is known, has a long history in the United States. Pennsylvania enacted arbitration legislation more than fifty years ago. Other states, such as Florida and Hawaii, have followed suit with good success. During a recent year in Hawaii, 86 percent of the cases brought to arbitration never went to court.

The practice of ADR consists of five closely related skills.

+ *Arbitration* means submitting a dispute to a third party, who renders a judgment after hearing arguments and reviewing evidence. Ordinarily the process is binding, although in some instances a losing party may still take a case to trial.

+ *Mediation* is the more complex process of trying to help disputing parties resolve their differences and come to an agreement. It's often used with combatants who have ongoing relationships, such as next-door neighbors or divorcing parents.

✦ *Mediation/arbitration* is an attempt to resolve as many problems as possible through mediation, referring the rest to arbitration.

✦ *Facilitation* is a more informal approach to less serious problems: a method of consensus-building.

✦ *Negotiation* is an even more basic skill. It's the art of give and take in the ordinary conflicts of life.

From the tone of those descriptions, it's evident how different alternative dispute resolution is from the traditional practice of law. ADR is built on skills of communication rather than disputation. It's based on a faith that, as the late Senator Everett Dirksen observed, "The oil can is mightier than the sword."

Part of the effectiveness of ADR may be that its skills tend to blend with other kinds of expertise. Those who have trained as practitioners come from many walks of life: realtors, engineers, construction managers, engineers, architects, college professors of industrial relations, physicians, and marriage and family therapists, as well as attorneys.

But the portability of alternative dispute resolution skills has had a downside. While enlarging other occupations, ADR skills by and large have not created a profession of their own. Two years after the Shortridges and their partner founded Arbitration Mediation Associates, they were forced to shut it down for lack of income. Shortridge went back to the traditional practice of law. This pattern can be seen throughout the country. The fact is, alternative dispute resolution has become more of an art than a profession. It's a collection of skills that complement some other way of making a living. For example, an arbitrator skilled in construction management may be especially effective in resolving a dispute between a home owner and a contractor. A marriage therapist may be qualified to serve as a mediator in a case of child custody. (Most therapists serve as mediators with the clients of other clinicians rather than their own.)

For the most part, then, ADR works best as an add-on skill. However, there are a few public- and private-sector fields where full-time jobs are developing. Government agencies are hiring ombudsmen to help resolve disputes with constituents in conflict-prone areas where statutes have been unclear or ineffective. In Colorado, workmen's compensation laws have caused headaches for years. The state recently hired a half-dozen ombudsmen to help mediate disputes.

Corporations are hiring ombudsmen, too—or assigning existing staff with special training to the positions. Membership in the Corporate Ombudsmen Association has more than doubled in four years.

As a whole, the field of ADR—including part-time practitioners—has grown rapidly. SPIDR, the Society of Professionals in Dispute Resolution, had two hundred members in 1971. In 1991 it had two thousand.

Preventive Law

Other lawyers have found their way to the field of "preventive law." The American Corporate Counsel Association has been adding 1,500 new members a year for a decade. For those who don't relish litigation, in-house law offers the appeal of working to prevent lawsuits. It's a field that draws more on research than trial skills.

Some attorneys have tried to meld those skills into a new legal specialty. Edward Dauer, a professor and former dean at the University of Denver Law School, has been a leader in efforts to help lawyers head off conflict. He says, "Most attorneys don't know how to deliver services prior to some disaster." Dauer, who believes in legal health, says most people could benefit from a periodic "legal checkup," not unlike a physical checkup. Did you just get married? Or buy a condominium? You have new legal circumstances. Or suppose you just turned eighteen. At age seventeen or younger, one may return a used car for a full refund. After eighteen, one can't. That's the kind of issue lawyers could help clients review in advance.

One of the problems with preventive law is its expense. Simply drawing up a checklist of lurking disasters could send clients into bankruptcy. But in certain common problem areas, such as drawing up wills or providing advance instructions for medical treatment, preventive law materials are becoming more common. Some of the most popular materials are computer-based.

Negotiation

Of all the skills in alternative dispute resolution, negotiation may have the broadest currency. Like assertiveness, humor, team-building, and delegation, the ability to negotiate agreements is a skill that serves well for our entire lives and contributes to our growth as whole persons.

Herb Cohen, author of *You Can Negotiate Anything*, has made a career of the subject. Cohen is a big, burly businessman who seems to thrive on negotiation. Perhaps the most entertaining lecturer I've ever heard, he spins out stories of Yiddish folk wisdom in the borscht-circuit style of a stand-up comic.

Cohen believes that negotiation is an interactive process whose purpose is to open options rather than close them. It begins with the way we formulate problems. Always frame issues, says Cohen, so that you broaden choices rather than narrow them. The purpose is to create an environment where problems can be solved. Start with areas of agreement rather than conflict. Talk about things you have in common. Save conflictual material for the end.

When problems come up, ask questions rather than raise complaints. If a proposal is so outlandish that you can't frame a question, just grunt: "Huh?" or "Wha-?" Keep the dialogue low-key and flowing, with an image of calculated incompetence.

One of Cohen's role models is Ronald Reagan, whom he served as an advisor. He believes that Reagan's greatest strength as a negotiator was that he came off as a congenial bungler—someone who only half-heard Sam Donaldson's weekly question as he climbed aboard the helicopter to Camp David, but could always be counted on for a wave and a smile.

Jimmy Carter, another of Cohen's clients, was much less effective, because he tried to present himself as super-competent in negotiations. Carter was a diligent student of foreign affairs who, Cohen believes, overprepared when trying to resolve the hostage crisis in Iran.

"He probably knew the Ayatollah Khomeini's birthday," says Cohen. "And he always took care to pronounce his name correctly, like he was coughing." That's bad negotiation, he maintains. It's better to come off as a bungler.

Cohen believes in taking notes, both to indicate that one is paying attention and also to pin down the details of an agreement. He quotes Marilyn Monroe on that subject: "The faintest ink is better than the fondest memory."

Alternatives for Attorneys

For those who are considering negotiating a radical change right out of law, there are other resources. Matt Resnik, an outplacement counselor, has developed a specialized practice in career alternatives for attorneys. His business has been brisk as law firms have been downsizing.

Resnik has come to several conclusions about the needs and abilities of attorneys. "Lawyers are great at research and analysis," he says. "They love anything that calls for a logical progression of thought.

"Where many of them are hurting is in social skills. That's bad, in a tight economy where the ability to generate new business is crucial. But many people in this field are socially isolated. They've been able to insulate themselves with power and money.

"Generally, the rainmakers who thrive on client contacts are still doing fine. It's the back-office people, cranking out the work, who are in trouble."

Resnik has spent an increasing amount of time with associates who have failed to make partner. These new professionals, who are hired out of law school, generally serve four to seven years before being considered for promotion to partner. They're paid well; $50,000 to $60,000 annual salaries are common. But they're also expected to generate anywhere from 1,600 to 1,800 billable hours per year. That can translate to an average eighty-hour work week.

Resnik finds that some of his clients who have lost their jobs are basically well-balanced people who don't want to pour themselves into their profession. In many cases, they'd failed to understand what they'd got themselves into.

"Law students may have images of wood-paneled offices and country clubs," he says. "What they miss seeing is that associates sit in libraries hour after hour, researching and filling out forms."

He tries to help displaced attorneys take stock of what they really want in a career, assess the skills they have to offer, and research market conditions in other sectors of the economy.

Some of his clients who've opted to stay in law have found jobs in small "boutique" firms that concentrate on a single specialty, such as water rights. That can be a way to bring one's career into focus. A few have become managers of litigation services for corporations. That's an emerging role designed to control corporate legal expenses by shopping around for the best deal on services. Others try to "hybridize" their legal training with skills from another, related field such as real estate or banking. It's a way to build a new niche in a nine-to-five job with realistic hours and a new lifestyle in the bargain.

Resources

SPIDR, the Society for Professionals in Dispute Resolution, can be reached at (714) 963-7114. *The Corporate Ombudsmen Association* is at (202) 458-1056. *The Center for Dispute Resolution*, which provides short-term courses in ADR, is at 100 Arapahoe Street, Suite 12, Boulder, Colorado 80302. Phone: (303) 442-7367.

Cohen's book, *You Can Negotiate Anything*, is published by Bantam for $4.95. *Getting to Yes* is another popular title, by Roger Fisher and William Ury (Penguin, $8.95).

For a fresh perspective on alternatives to legal careers, see *Running from the Law* (Ten Speed Press, $11.95). It's a popular book among attorneys in search of options.

Chapter Seven

Association Management and Other Roles in Reorganized Labor

Imagine an industry that grows at the rate of 10 percent a year, where the ranks of top managers have doubled in the past decade. That's the association industry in America.

The remarkable growth of associations is rooted in one of the major transitions in today's economy: the movement I call "reorganized labor."

Most of us associate the phrase "organized labor" with America's traditional labor unions—those blue-collar groups that seem to be fading away with the old industrial economy. Labor unions have lost so many members in recent years that today more people own businesses than hold union cards. But that doesn't mean organized labor is dead. There is, in fact, a remarkable amount of organization occurring among American workers. It's the reorganization of entrepreneurs in small-business incubators, franchising organizations, and temporary employment services, as well as professional associations. Each of these groups, like associations, has been growing steadily throughout the 1980s. In this chapter we'll look at each of these organizations, not only as support systems for entrepreneurs, but also as significant sources of employment.

✦ ✦ ✦

Association Management

Americans always have been a society of joiners. But today the associations they're forming are different from the fraternal groups of the past. They're more like schools than social gatherings, taking on many of the training functions the changing economy requires. They are also advocacy groups. They're beginning to fulfill some of the same political functions that traditional labor unions have performed. In addition, they're serving as networks for collaborative buying and other shared services, such as health insurance. Associations are potentially powerful organizations.

Consider these numbers. *The Encyclopedia of Associations* is a comprehensive directory of information on all sorts of organizations in the United States. It's an immense publication: four volumes in all. In 1986 the *Encyclopedia* listed eighteen thousand entries. In 1991 it had twenty-two thousand. That's an increase of 32 percent in five years.

Here's a second example of the growth rate. The American Society of Association Executives is a professional organization for those who manage organizations. In 1986 the ASAE had twelve thousand members. In 1991 they had twenty thousand: up 66 percent over five years. That's how fast associations are growing.

The reason for that growth, as we've seen, is that America's economy, which for twenty-five years after World War II was based on large corporations and labor organizations, is fast becoming a new economy of entrepreneurs. Actually, as William Ouchi, author of *Theory Z*, has pointed out, the development is not so new. For most of its history the United States has been a nation of independent professionals and small-business owners. Today's new economy may simply be a rebirth of the original version.

Professional associations are at the heart of this movement. They're forming in every conceivable field. One of the fastest-growing groups in recent years is an association of video-rental-store owners. As one veteran association director told me, "Anything you might be wearing or eating or driving, there's an association for it."

Most established associations in the United States tend to cluster around Washington, D.C. That's partly because of their lobbying activities, and partly because clustered associations can reduce costs by sharing suppliers in printing and other basic services, as well as research and staff. There are some good-sized clusters in other cities too. Most associations are footloose groups that can locate just about anywhere. In some cases, the groups have created their own business environment; they're attracted by one another's presence.

When it comes to careers in associations, the first concern, of course, is to find a group large enough to afford an office and professional staff. Many associations are staffed solely by volunteers. Others may contract with a firm that manages the affairs of several small organizations. Those companies are found in most major cities under the heading "Association Management" in the telephone Yellow Pages.

Often the first paid director of an association is a member of the group who's risen from the ranks of volunteers. That's a significant transition, as is usually the case with any move into management. On the one hand, the member-turned-director may know everyone in the organization well. But as paid staff, that person's relationship with others in the group will change.

Several years ago I interviewed an experienced association manager who was serving half time as coordinator of a statewide organization of nonprofits and the other half as director of a manufacturers' association. That's a typical, jury-rigged arrangement for two groups that can't quite fund an independent operation.

I asked the manager what kind of life he'd had in association work. "It's about like any other kind of business management," he said. "The only difference is that in association management you have a new boss every year when the elected officers change.

"Sometimes you're dealing with people who don't understand the boundaries of their roles. An officer may not recognize where his responsibility ends and yours begins. Then, too, sometimes when the economy goes into a downturn, you'll find members vying for your job."

His remarks were prophetic. The next time I met that manager, he was out of work and networking for a new job. Today he's back in the field as an independent consultant, managing the affairs of several small associations—still in the same career.

Perhaps that's typical of professionals in the field. As another manager commented, "Once you get association work in your blood, that's about all you want to do."

Association managers must be good generalists. Much of their work involves problem-solving in a wide range of subjects, including the law. In recent years, for instance, the Internal Revenue Service has tightened regulations on nonprofit organizations, enforcing payment of something called Unrelated Business Income Taxes. Those are levies on income from the sale of advertising in convention programs, for example. If those tax bills accumulate and the IRS discovers the backlog, an association can go under.

Tax-law revisions, plus the decade-long 1980s recession, have posed a double-barreled threat to one important segment of the nonprofit field: charitable organizations. When tax deductions for charitable contributions were reduced in 1986, donations by America's wealthiest families fell by two-thirds in a period of just two years. As a result, some analysts believe that 5 to 10 percent of America's nonprofits may not survive the current recession. The most vulnerable organizations are the "C-3s," which provide services to people who can't pay for them, such as the homeless. (They hold 501(c)(3) status with the IRS.) Three-quarters of such groups have annual budgets of less than $25,000. This kind of vulnerability presents an extra set of challenges to anyone looking to manage a charitable organization.

Skills needed for association management include accounting and finance, marketing and fund-raising, publications and public re-- lations, personnel management, and staff development, as well as the recruitment and management of volunteers. In all, nonprofit management calls for all the skills of business management and more. Keeping a voluntary membership association afloat is probably more demanding than any leadership role in the profit sector. As Carol Barbeito, a consultant in nonprofit management, observes, "This really isn't something just everybody should do if they've been a manager. Often the general manager of a nonprofit is the only manager."

She recommends that those who change careers into the nonprofit sector not try to start out at the head of an association, but use a transferable technical skill, such as accounting and computer operations, to move into the lower echelons of the organization. The ability to manage volunteers or to market a "soft product," such as social services, also make good transferable skills.

Meeting planning is another interesting bridge between the profit and nonprofit sectors. As we'll see in chapter 17, "Tourism and Transportation," planning conventions and conferences has become a thriving worldwide industry, with revenues on the order of two trillion dollars a year. In the United States, professional meetings are now as large an industry as higher education: some 35 billion dollars per year. Today, a typical hotel earns half its revenue from conferences.

I met Cynthia Gleason, a meeting-planning specialist, when she was arranging a series of impressive business-development seminars for General Electric. "From a public-relations standpoint," she told me, "planning an event requires three skills. First you must understand your client's needs and objectives. What is their event intended to accomplish?

"Then you need to know your community. What kinds of events will people turn out for? Finally you must have a strong sense of detail. Meeting planning means covering every possible eventuality. How many drinks will you serve? What will you do if a speaker doesn't show up?"

While large firms and associations hire specialists such as Gleason to stage events, most groups will expect association managers to provide those skills. It's just one more competence in a generalist's field. Roger Kahn, a former community organizer for the Congress of Racial Equality (CORE), runs a degree program in nonprofit administration. He describes the skills he teaches as "everything you learn in the process of trying to advance a cause with limited resources."

As one might imagine, salaries for association executives range all over the map. I've found full-time directors making anywhere from $18,000 to $100,000 per year. A 1991 survey of 225 member organizations in the Colorado Society of Association Executives drew ninety-seven responses. The average annual salary of those managers was $55,000. Several reported having received pay raises of 33 percent in the past year.

Board Membership

For those who are less concerned with income than with making good use of their free time, such as America's millions of early retirees, serving on the board of an association can be a valuable experience. If board members are well prepared for their responsibilities, the associations can benefit as well. According to Nancy Kinne, who directed a training program for board members, "Nonprofit organizations go through two phases in recruiting board members. First they tend to look for people who understand the need they're trying to address, whether it's homelessness, illiteracy, or supporting the arts.

"Then, if the organization prospers, they find they're in need of other kinds of skills: usually technical assistance in anything from accounting to marketing to law. We call that growth phase 'managing the mushroom.'"

For example, a board member with experience in fund-raising may understand that no organization should base more than 50 percent of its income on a single source, such as a fund-raising event. And someone with legal expertise may be able to advise board members of the limits of their liability, should the organization go under. Several years ago, an employment service for displaced homemakers folded when an annual fund-raising event that was its sole source of revenue failed two years in a row. After the organization went defunct, the board members discovered that their director had paid no federal payroll taxes for several years. Those taxes turned out to be a non-negotiable obligation to the IRS, for which the board members were responsible.

It's no wonder that interest in nonprofit management training has been steadily rising.

Franchising

Franchising is another fast-growing form of reorganized labor. At last count there were five hundred thousand franchise owners in the U.S. They employed eight million people in sixty different industries and accounted for one-third of all retail revenues in the nation.

Franchisers sell business acumen. They're bright individuals such as Mance Etheredge, a sign painter who invented a way to apply computer technology to sign making. In the early 1980s, Etheredge was introduced to computer plotters: high-tech graphic-printing devices. He deduced that the same technology that created images on $8\frac{1}{2}$-by-11 pages could be used for large signs as well. Before long, he'd founded a nationwide company, Signs Now, to franchise his concept. Today there are more than a hundred Signs Now stores across the country.

One of my favorite success stories in franchising is the case of my college friend, Tom Christensen, who in mid-life became a student of Etheredge's new technology. Christensen had spent most of his career in the field of human services. He was director of the largest private social-service agency in metropolitan St. Louis.

At age fifty, one of those deadline decades when people tend to take stock of their circumstances, he decided that he was tired of dealing with fund-raising and volunteer recruitment. "It's time to do something for myself," he said.

Now in his fifth year of business, Christensen owns two stores and employs a dozen workers. He's considering adding a third store and is constantly experimenting with new technology and testing new markets with the support of his franchisers—Fast Signs, a competitor of Etheredge's firm. While the venture has been filled with risk (Christensen and his wife mortgaged their house to finance it), developing the stores and learning Etheredge's sign-making technology has revitalized a fifty-year-old who needed a new direction.

Christensen advises prospective franchise owners to do their homework: "Study the daylights out of a business before you jump in." He suggests several areas on which to focus.

+ First there's the industry. Is there a need for the kind of business you're considering, in the community where you want to operate it? Talk with some of your prospective competitors. Are they doing well enough to consider expanding?

+ Then, consider your background. Franchising is a business of sweat-equity. Are you ready to put in double-digit hours every day for the first few years? Do you know anything

about the kind of business you're considering? Have you pa-
tronized it? Do you enjoy it?

✦ Consider your finances. Franchises can cost anywhere from
$300,000 (for a restaurant) to less than $100,000 for a pack-
aging and shipping store. Buyers are expected to put up at
least 20 percent of the purchase price. In addition to the
franchise fee, you'll need operating capital until the business becomes profitable.

✦ Finally, investigate the franchiser. Who are the founders?
Are they the current owners? Where have they done business, and how successful have they been?

Don't confuse visibility with success. Some fast-growing franchising operatives have profited by selling franchises to all comers,
regardless of whether they're doing business across the street from
an existing franchiser. As a result, many of their franchisees have
gone under. Territory rights are a vitally important factor in any franchise agreement. Franchisers are required to provide a prospectus of
their business, covering this and other arrangements.

"The quality of franchisers runs the gamut," says Christensen.
"I asked one of them for his mission statement. He told me: 'To
make money.' That was it. He had no vision. The company I finally
signed with had a mission statement written in their strategic plan."

Find out what services the franchiser will provide, advises
Christensen. That includes site location, product research, and
whether you're buying into a start-up or long-term relationship. Ask
to see a copy of the training manual.

"Then prepare to learn what you don't know. Find yourself a
good accountant, lawyer, and banker."

While franchises represent a large share of America's burgeoning new businesses, which have increased seven-fold in the past
forty years, not everyone is attracted to the idea of selling someone
else's proven product. Some people want to bring their own ideas to
market.

For that sort of inventive entrepreneur, small-business incubators offer another kind of learning environment.

Small-business Incubators

Incubators offer support services, such as copy machines, microcomputers, and receptionists, to fledgling firms. Equally important,
they provide education and counseling in business-development
skills such as marketing, finance, and accounting. The services are

intended to help inventors who are stronger in creativity than in management skills.

Carlos Morales, president of the National Business Incubator Association, believes that quite a few business owners need that kind of help. Often, he says, "entrepreneurs are working off more emotion than common sense. They are taking a huge risk, emotionally and usually financially. My favorite definition of an entrepreneur is someone who goes out on the end of a limb with a piece of paper and a pencil and then draws more limbs." That's where an incubator can help innovators build skills as business generalists.

As an institution, incubators are a recent invention, only about ten years old. But their numbers have been growing about 15 percent a year. That's because of their track record. Whereas typically 80 percent of new businesses fail within the first five years, for businesses in incubators the ratio is reversed. Four of five incubator-based businesses succeed, as do 95 percent of franchise-supported businesses.

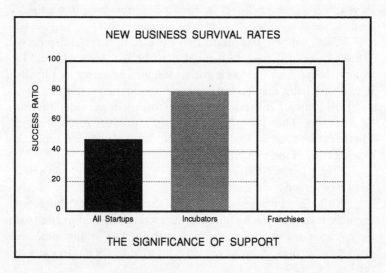

NEW BUSINESS SURVIVAL RATES

THE SIGNIFICANCE OF SUPPORT

Incubators are usually sponsored by government agencies, proprietary firms such as AT&T or Control Data (which originated the concept), or by universities interested in commercializing their research. The latest trends are for incubators to be founded for profit and for export. Many Eastern European countries are looking into the incubator model as a resource for new market economies.

Some predict that there will be a thousand incubators in the United States by the turn of the century. That kind of growth should create an abundance of new jobs in incubator management, and a more formal profession in the process. For now, the people who are managing incubators are career changers who have demonstrated managerial skills and who basically come from all over. Most seem to be doing an excellent job of teaching inventors to survive in business.

Not everyone, of course, is cut out to manage an organization or start a new business. But there are other alternatives in the world of reorganized labor.

Take temporary employment services.

Temporary Employment Services

The temp industry originated during World War II, when American employers were scrambling for workers. But it was in the early 1970s, when American firms began to reduce core staff, that they really began to grow. The number of services has increased by an average 10 percent annually for twenty years. Today there are ten thousand temp service offices nationwide, and they employ over ten million workers.

Temporary services are sometimes confused with employment agencies that act on behalf of workers or employers. But they are in fact a different entity, and that's why they've grown so fast. Temporary service companies serve as an employer of record: recruiting, screening, and sometimes even paying benefits to their employees. They relieve their client firms of all the hassles of hiring.

The other point of confusion about temp services has to do with workers. Most people assume that the services employ only short-term workers for low-grade office jobs—that all temps are hunt-and-peck typists who merely answer phones and brew coffee.

Admittedly, part of that scenario still is true. Temporary workers do mostly take short-term jobs; the average tenure per job is about a month and a half. And to match another stereotype, 75 percent of temporary employees are female.

But the work these people are doing is changing markedly. Most positions today are nonclerical. Many are in manufacturing and health care. An increasing number of jobs are professional, as are the workers. Today, 35 percent of temporary workers hold college degrees.

Temporary services can now be found that specialize in accounting, law, computer services, and health care. One firm I know of employs only nurses; the company is owned by a group of nurses. Another company hires physicians for short-term assignments in rural areas; another employs only lawyers. The trend toward specialization, in turn, has sparked a related interest in training. Most temporary services today offer self-study tutorial programs in popular computer software. For someone who's conversant with a particular computer application, such as word processing in WordStar, but wants to learn a new program such as WordPerfect, signing on with a temporary service may be a good route to fast, free training.

Some firms are going so far as to offer classes in specific computer operations. Several years ago, Sue and Ken Petracek teamed with their friend, Mitzi Gibson, to open a temporary agency called Maccess. Sue and Mitzi both have degrees in education and thought they saw a market opportunity to offer classes for temporary workers in Macintosh software. The classes are open to the public but are offered at reduced rates to their roster of two hundred temps. They cover a half-dozen different software functions: file management, word processing, accounting, spreadsheet financial planning, desktop publishing, and electronic mail. With that kind of skill base, Maccess temporaries can walk into a Macintosh-equipped office and not miss a beat.

For workers, the combination of classes with work experience offers a solid foundation in a cluster of integrated skills. It's a great way to increase one's value on the open market.

As it happens, though, Maccess employees tend to stay with the firm about twice as long as the national average of 4.6 weeks. Learning is ongoing, as Apple continues to offer new software programs for the Macintosh. And the process of developing skills together builds loyalty.

The workers, of course, begin studies at different levels. Many ex-corporate employees are conversant with the Macintosh but have used the computer for only one function. Some of the best temps at Maccess are recent college graduates who learned to use the Macintosh in school. Not long ago the firm hired a married couple who had just completed law school and needed a source of income as they studied for bar exams. It's a good example of how temporary employment services can help shore up the careers of white-collar professionals.

Resources

One of the best-known programs in nonprofit management is the **Center for Leadership Development**, a series of courses sponsored by the National Chamber Foundation, an organization of chambers of commerce. Their address is 1615 H Street, N.W., Washington, D.C. 20062. Phone: (202) 463-5570.

The American Society of Association Executives is another good resource. Their address is The ASAE Building, 1575 I Street, N.W., Washington, D.C. 20062. Phone: (202) 626-2727. One of their principal publications is *Principles of Association Management: A Professional's Handbook.*

For local training opportunities, look for the statewide "**association of associations**" in your area. The ASAE is a good source of information. Local chapters of the **United Way** frequently offer training programs as well.

A good, comprehensive book on the subject of meeting planning is *The AMA Guide for Meeting and Event Planners* by Catherine Price. The book is a $75 reference text published by the American Management Association. To order, call the AMA at (518) 891-5510.

For a basic introduction, see *How to Organize and Manage a Seminar* by Sheila Murray (Prentice Hall, $8.95).

The principal association in the field is **Meeting Planners International.** Their address is Infomart, Suite 5018, 1950 Stemmons Freeway, Dallas, Texas 75270-3109. Phone: (214) 712-7700.

For more information on franchising, contact the International Franchise Association at 1350 New York Avenue, N.W., Suite 900, Washington, D.C. 20005. Phone: (202) 628-8000. Their *Franchising Opportunities Guide* sells for $14, including shipping and handling.

For additional information on small-business incubators, contact the **National Business Incubator Association** at One President Street, Athens, Ohio 45701. Phone: (614) 593-4331.

For more information on trends and educational opportunities in the temporary employment field, contact the **National Association of Temporary Services** at 119 South Asaph Street, Alexandria, Virginia 22314. Phone: (703) 549-6287.

Chapter Eight

Business and Technical Communications

In a society where there's more to know every day but less time to learn it, the business of communication is taking on more importance. Studies today show that communications of all kinds, from phone calls to letters, are becoming shorter and that audiences for printed matter are becoming more clearly defined.

That's why interest in business and technical communications is surging. Membership in the Society for Technical Communication has been growing at 8 to 10 percent a year for the past five years. This chapter offers sketches of current developments in these fields, plus some sage advice on educational planning in new industries.

> *"There is so much information we can't process it all.*
> *The information is like a constant avalanche that never*
> *ends, never runs out of snow . . . . There is too damned*
> *much intelligence and we are drowning in it."*
> — BILL GRANGER, *There Are No Spies*

◆　◆　◆

The quote is from a novel about espionage, but it's hard to find a field it doesn't fit. Computer technology has multiplied the amount of printed material in circulation today, but fewer people are keeping up with it. A study conducted at MIT a few years ago found that printed matter had increased three times faster than the capacity of readers to digest it. Add to that the fact that television is reducing the ranks of those who enjoy reading at all—household newspaper subscriptions have decreased 20 percent in the past twenty years—and you begin to sense that writers have a serious challenge on their hands.

While some would argue that television and other electronic media may substitute for print, providing more palatable access to the same kinds of information, that doesn't always seem to be the case. Technological products today are increasingly complex. And so is the information required to explain them. Most of us still need printed instructions.

Take the field of automotive technology. Today's high-revving engines and on-board computers have revolutionized the business of servicing cars. That's why General Motors' new manuals for automotive technicians require reading levels ranging from tenth grade to the senior year of college.

Or consider your own experience the last time you bought a high-tech appliance. Remember trying to decipher the owner's manual? You wished the VCR had come with a college-trained genie.

Across the country, a number of colleges and professional groups are beginning to address the problem of communicating in a complex society where literacy levels are falling. Together they're creating all sorts of stimulating techniques in the field of business and technical communication. Here are a couple of examples.

Jim Hunt is a specialist in workplace communication. It's a field he entered only recently after twenty years as an English teacher in the public schools. Hunt is a high-wired, effusive man with a quick wit and a gift for language. He's exactly the kind of person who makes a memorable high school teacher. But after twenty years, he needed a change.

Hunt had done some part-time evening teaching at a banking institute. He taught business English and enjoyed helping mid-life workers develop their communication skills. But business English didn't tap the deeper reaches of his creativity. Then one night at the banking institute, someone came to him for help with a newsletter. He loved putting the newsletter together. Suddenly a vision of his new career direction appeared in life-sized, living color.

Hunt began to do research on newsletters. He discovered that there are sixty thousand newsletters published in the United States. The numbers have been growing with the rise in special interest groups. Newsletters are a customized product for niche audiences. The micro-publishing equivalent of cable television channels, they provide a direct link with a targeted audience.

They are not, however, widely read. Surveys show that only 5 percent of newsletters are unwrapped before they hit the trash can. Most of what's read is only scanned. Studies indicate that, while 100 percent of readers will look at headlines and photographs in a newsletter, and 70 percent will digest bold-faced print and highlighted quotes, only 5 to 30 percent will read the text.

Part of the problem may be the content of the publications. A survey of in-house publications by the International Association of Business Communicators suggests that many editors fail to connect with the needs and interests of their constituencies. Of every hundred articles published, only twenty-five targeted issues of interest to employers who were footing the bill for the publication—such as product development, quality assurance, and keeping up with new technology. Employees' concerns, such as the company's future or opportunities for career advancement, were not addressed with much more regularity. Yet the publications were a major expense. The typical annual budget for a company publication is $100,000 to $200,000.

Hunt found that most newsletter editors are not particularly qualified or committed to their job. Most are reluctant volunteers, or staff members who have been assigned to produce a newsletter without prior training. So he set about designing a course, "Writing and Editing Your Organization's Newsletter," and began offering it at lunch hour to workers in the local business district. It has been a great success.

The first topic he covers is "defining your audience." Hunt finds there are three kinds of newsletters on the market today.

+ *House organs* are publications intended to build morale in an organization by sharing personal information about employees. Here, the folksier the style, the better. "Joannie had her baby." "Bob got back from Florida, and boy, is he tan!"

+ Then there's the *newsletter-as-brochure.* Today, many struggling white-collar professionals such as doctors, dentists, and lawyers are publishing newsletter promos with information updates in their fields. It's a veiled form of advertising.

+ Finally there are *common-interest newsletters*, published for a group of individuals who pursue the same hobby and/or belong to the same organization, such as quilters or members of a fan club or a church.

According to Hunt, these purebred newsletters are the easiest to write, given the base of common interests. It's the house organs and promotional newsletters that require special skills, skills ranging from sales to seduction. Editors must find ways to interest people in writing for and reading the publications.

One of the best strategies for editors, Hunt says, is to make themselves a clearing-house for information rather than originating every story. Another is simply to write interesting stories with some snap and sparkle. "When you write these days," he says, "you have to imagine that your reader has a remote control device in his hand. If he doesn't read your story right now, he probably won't read it."

Finally there's the matter of page design. Desktop publishing programs have made it possible to print colorful copy with all sorts of embellishments. But it's easily overdone. Use more than three type styles per page, and your newsletter will look like a combination pizza.

Desktop publishing is a deceptive technology. Production quality has improved so much that it's often difficult to distinguish in-house publications from the work of professional printers. But the technology requires training in graphic design. That's why most of the best desktop publishing programs offer more than instruction in the software. They include courses in layout, design, and typography.

Many community colleges and vocational schools go into the subject at good depth. A few years ago I visited a technical communications class at a two-year college. Half the students there already had degrees from four-year institutions. That's a typical pattern in community colleges, where the emphasis is on short-term training in marketable skills.

The students were a diverse lot. One was a chemist who wanted to escape a job in laboratory management. Another was a medical illustrator with a degree in biology. Then there was Dianne Gregory, a one-time high-school English teacher who had burned out, as Jim Hunt had, and at about the same age. Gregory, age forty-two, wanted a less demanding job with clearly defined hours. That's why technical communications appealed to her.

So did the idea of earning a certificate in the field, even though she already had a more advanced degree. She said, "At my age, I need a credential. I need a straight line to something." Gregory got a job writing specifications for field engineers at a computer software company.

Technical communications is one of those rapidly changing fields where one should exercise caution when it comes to degrees. Checking employment figures a few years ago, I found there were about 120,000 Americans employed in the industry. Most had been trained on the job. Of seventy college programs in technical communication, only ten had been in existence for as long as five years.

Obviously the academic institutions were late-comers who had trained only a small fraction of the practitioners in the field. Yet when I interviewed faculty and administrators at several local college programs, I heard all sorts of blue-sky stories of what one could do with a degree in the field. Some universities were even persuading students to sign up for graduate degrees. That's dangerous in a field that's populated by practitioners with little formal training. It's another instance of colleges' and universities' setting up credentialing systems that may be more self-serving than beneficial to students. In technical communications, as in any new field, it makes sense to begin by taking small clusters of skills in clearly-defined fields such as newsletter production or desktop publishing.

Many community colleges and adult continuing-education programs offer certificate programs for, say, a half-dozen courses in technical communication. That's often a good way to begin, particularly if students are simultaneously developing an internship or some other job link with the new field. Then, as one gains some entry-level skills and gets the lay of the land, it's possible to make some solid decisions about additional training. Volunteering with a social service agency can be a good way to learn newsletter production, and sometimes desktop publishing as well.

One of the late-breaking stories in business communication involves the use of new telecommunications technology to share and filter information. Confertech, a new company that specializes in conference calling, is marketing an audio newsletter to stockbrokers.

To appreciate their sales pitch, imagine an investment advisor trying to update clients in a constantly-changing market. Stockbrokers have serious information overload problems. They could be on the phone all the time.

Then picture an audio newsletter.

Here's how it works. A financial advisor schedules a half-hour conference call once a week—say, every Monday afternoon. Clients call the broker's 800 number and are patched in to the audio conference. (With modern technology, over 1,000 participants can be connected in a single conference call.)

The broker can distribute background printed matter by "blast fax" before the call begins, or follow-up material afterward. During the call itself, participants can line up to ask questions by pressing a button on their phones. Using the same queuing technology, they also can be asked to register opinions on developments in the market.

If some clients have to miss the call, they simply dial in afterward for a recording of it. Again, using advanced audio technology they can fast-forward and rewind through the material, just as they'd review a tape cassette.

While the teleconferencing market thus far has only a few players (AT&T is dominant), it's creating some interesting new job roles. At Confertech, operators are called "conference administrators." They work at a hybrid telephone/computer device called "the bridge." Their job is referred to as "running the bridge." It calls for good technical skills to master the equipment.

In addition, the administrators need good diction and high energy levels. They also must be sensitive to each of the industry and professional groups who are using conference calls these days (including physicians, pharmaceutical houses, lawyers, and bankers). They need to understand what each group is seeking from the system.

In addition to conference administrators, Confertech employs a staff of reservationists who set up the calls and a substantial group of computer hardware and software engineers to develop and maintain the equipment.

Audio newsletters and other forms of conference calling are an example of new businesses that could emerge from revolutionary developments in the telecommunications industry.

Resources

For more information on the field of technical communications, contact:

The Society for Technical Communication, 901 North Stuart Street, Suite 304, Arlington, Virginia 22203. Phone: (703) 522-4114.

The International Association of Business Communicators, One Hallidie Plaza, Suite 600, San Francisco, California 94102. Phone: (415) 433-3400.

The Public Relations Society of America, 33 Irving Place, New York, New York 10003. Phone: (212) 995-2230.

A number of books on the market provide an introduction to newsletter production and desktop publishing. One of them is *Newsletters from the Desktop: Designing Effective Publications With Your Computer*, by Roger C. Parker. It's published by Ventana Press at $23.95.

Chapter Nine

Business Management

Management is working with others to get things done. In that sense, given an economy where organizations are constantly changing, *managerial skills* may be more valuable than ever.

But *management as a profession* is another matter. As pyramid organizations turn diamond-shaped, traditional corporate management jobs are shrinking. Those are the jobs where managers specialized in supervising the work of others. As corporations downsize, those full-time managers often are the first let go.

That's why managerial careers today are risky business, and call for careful planning.

Where are the jobs for managers? What skills are required, and how are they changing? Where is the best training? In this chapter, we'll explore those questions and consider new trends in the evolving field of business management.

◆　◆　◆

So You Wanna Be a Manager . . .

It was ten years ago, but Marty McNulty remembers the meeting as though it were yesterday. In 1982, the top officers of Public Service Company of Colorado, a regional utilities company, had assembled for a day of long-range, strategic planning. It was their annual gathering to take stock of the previous year and set goals for the future. As part of the meeting, McNulty and the other corporate officers always made decisions about personnel and promotions.

On this day, they faced a critical decision. One of Public Service's division heads was about to retire. The officers spent a long time studying their personnel files, deliberating over who should replace him. Finally they reached consensus and picked a promising young man who headed a Public Service office in rural Colorado.

One of the executives was sent to call him up and tell him the good news.

The messenger was gone a long time.

Finally, he returned with some shocking news. The young man had turned down the promotion! It seemed he didn't want to be a corporate manager. For several minutes, the executives sat in stunned silence. No one had conceived of such a possibility, and no one knew what to do.

For McNulty, that was a watershed experience. He sensed it was time to develop some new approaches to personnel selection. Instead of drawing up career succession plans and charting each employee's next move, perhaps they ought to begin by asking people where *they* thought they should go.

McNulty's radical idea took hold. He spend the next decade building a Career Planning Department at Public Service, to help workers decide whether they're cut out for managerial careers. He's learned to take a cautious view of managerial careers. McNulty has come to believe that most people give up as much as they gain if they accept a promotion into management. It's a transition he calls "the vital shift." For one thing, managers must give up the satisfaction of working independently—turning out a product with their own hands—in order to spend their time helping others be productive instead.

In newspapers, that means exchanging the role of writer for that of editor: reviewing other people's copy. In education, it means leaving the classroom for the principal's office—spending more time working with paper than with people.

McNulty offers a course, "Preview of Supervision," for would-be managers in his company. He targets three questions:

+ What is your motivation for going into management? "Beware of the three Ps," he advises. "If your motives are simply Power, Prestige, and a larger Paycheck, that's not enough."

+ Can you make the "vital shift," giving up seeing the product of your own hands in order to concentrate on the work of others?

+ Do you have enough flexibility to do the job? Can you use more than one interpersonal style—to wheedle, cajole, compliment, or ride herd on others as the occasion requires?

Above all, he asks, "Can you concentrate on giving those who report to you opportunities to grow?"

McNulty's system has been very effective; in recent years, employees who completed the Career Development Program were 33 percent more likely to receive managerial promotions than those who had not. It's the kind of program that would benefit other organizations and help workers make better career decisions.

Today, however, there are more questions facing managers than deciding whether to become one. The managerial role itself is changing. One of the major shifts is the "flattening" of organizations in which responsibilities have been shifted further down the ranks of workers. It's part of the development I have described as the diamond-shaped organization.

In personnel policies, the shift from pyramid to diamond organizations has led to smaller work units in which more responsibilities are shared. That has changed the role of manager from boss to coach. Many mid-career managers now find that the jobs they inherited have taken directions they never dreamed of.

New Roles for Managers

At the Adolph Coors Company, a brewery outside Denver, production workers once knew exactly where they stood. Workers were closely regulated in a top-down pyramid of authority. If an employee noticed that something was wrong in the production process—say, beer bottle labels were going on upside down—he had to leave his post and find a supervisor to stop the line. That could take ten minutes.

Today, under a new system of supervision, anyone may stop the line by summoning a co-worker and coming to a joint decision.

That's "empowerment," to cite a favorite buzz-word of management consultant Tom Peters. It was Peters who sold Peter Coors on the idea of pushing decisions to the lowest possible organizational level. Now production workers are organized into teams of ten, with each team responsible for its own schedules, production quotas, and quality control. The teams also participate in hiring decisions. While closely evaluated, they're eligible for bonuses and profit-sharing under the new system.

The system at Coors calls for new kinds of managers: supervisors who must work alongside—not over—the production employees. In fact, these management jobs are wedded so closely to production that it's hard to tell where one function ends and the other begins. It's a pattern that's seen in all sorts of American companies as traditional blue-collar jobs decline. Those are the routine production jobs that require close supervision. According to management analyst Peter Drucker, the traditional blue-collar workforce of General Motors has fallen from 85 percent to 25 percent since 1925. Today, blue-collar workers make up only 15 percent of the workforce at Ford, 18 percent at General Electric. The movement has upgraded the jobs of broadly-skilled manufacturing workers.

But empowering workers has played havoc with managerial careers. Coors eliminated an entire level of middle management jobs when they organized the new teams of production workers. The same process is occurring throughout the American workplace. Today, as the ranks of corporate managers thin and the blue-collar-to-white-collar career ladder crumbles, several different career paths are appearing. Here are several kinds of managerial careers.

Back to the Basics in Corporate Management

As long as there are corporations, there will, of course, be jobs for corporate managers. There will be accountants to keep books, public-relations directors to manage media relations, and strategic planners to decide where the organization is going. There will be middle managers who report to senior officers.

That's why pursuing a traditional career in corporate management is a realistic option—as long as one recognizes that there are fewer of those jobs to be had, and that the now-traditional rite of earning an MBA is not the smooth route to success it once was.

Choosing a business degree program is a serious decision these days, as the number of people with advanced degrees continues to mushroom. Currently, about seventy-five thousand MBAs are awarded each year. Both the number of degrees and the number of schools sponsoring MBA programs have doubled in the past twenty years.

The MBA is not a degree to seek just because everyone else is pursuing one.

For most people who are interested in a business management career, it makes more sense to concentrate on the basic skills of business. A good undergraduate degree in business will supply the essential skills needed in management. The core courses of accounting, finance, economics, marketing, and human resource management have retained value over the years.

Those skills are particularly valuable when combined with working knowledge of a particular industry. On the production line at Coors, for example, those who use managerial skills in team leadership must also know something about making beer. That's typical of many industries where management is being melded with operations in diamond-shaped organizations.

The shift is evident in companies such as Marty McNulty's

Public Service Company, where virtually every employee begins as either a meter-reader or a customer service representative. Similarly, at United Parcel Service, 'most everyone starts out delivering packages. Those kinds of career paths assure that those who take on greater management responsibilities understand what the basic business of the organization.

So for managerial careers within a large organization, it's a good idea to take the core courses of an undergraduate degree in business while gaining experience in the industry where one might like to work. The idea is to integrate one's experience and education, and keep them at the same pace.

New Options in Graduate Business Education

For those who *are* inclined to pursue a specialty in business and earn a graduate degree, there are some interesting new alternatives to the traditional MBA. One new approach that's appearing in certain MBA programs is the emphasis on the management of operations or production.

Gary Kochenberger, a professor at the University of Colorado at Denver's College of Business, is a specialist in **operations management**: the study of production methods in business. He developed an interest in the field growing up in Pueblo, Colorado—a small manufacturing city with a single large employer, CF&I Steel. Kochenberger's father spent forty-two years working for CF&I, before the United States lost much of its steel industry and massive layoffs occurred. In the 1970s, Pueblo suffered devastating unemployment. But local business leaders rallied to recruit a number of branch manufacturing plants to re-employ some of the laid-off steelworkers.

The new plants, such as Unisys and McDonnell Douglas, were a far cry from CF&I. Instead of rigid, top-down management systems, they used all kinds of innovative techniques to empower employees, as Coors is doing today. Kochenberger became enthralled by the new approaches to management and impressed by the importance of manufacturing.

"For twenty years," he says, "we've ignored how goods and services are produced, as opposed to how they're marketed or creatively financed. All the while, we've watched American competitiveness slip away. It's a sad commentary when people like Donald Trump, who never made a damned thing in his life, become our national heroes."

Kochenberger's courses in operations management include

production planning and control, purchasing and materials management, quality improvement, and operations strategy. The emphasis is on mathematical methods, such as statistical analysis and computer modeling, that can be applied to service industries as well as manufacturing. Some of his students are employees of ski resorts. They use computer modeling to explore new strategies for reducing the length of lift lines on the slopes.

Systems management is yet another new wrinkle in graduate business education. Here the emphasis is on the kinds of management skills required in technology-intensive organizations. Doug Johnson, a young manager with IBM, is one who has chosen to pursue a Master of Systems Management degree rather than an MBA. Johnson has one of those hybrid jobs that are becoming so common in the new economy. He's a "Systems Analyst and Ledger Coordinator." Translated, that means he spends his days helping IBM's computer systems and financial departments communicate. For Johnson, the purpose of continuing his education was to learn more about making advanced technology work within organizations.

The three main components of systems management are human factors (the study of how people interact with machines), organizational theory, and human resource management. Some believe the Challenger space shuttle disaster is a typical case study in the field: a classic example of slow reporting through encrusted layers of bureaucracy. The engineers who knew that seal rings in the Challenger booster rockets were faulty were unable to communicate with top decision makers until it was too late. Systems management students learn how to avoid that kind of problem by designing flatter organizations.

Another common problem is how to implement "concurrent engineering," where teams of technical specialists are required to work together in designing new products rather than proceeding step-by-step through layers of bureaucracy. Though concurrent engineering is clearly the wave of the future in modern manufacturing plants, most companies are still trying to learn how to make the system function.

Systems management is not a new field. It's actually about as old as the MBA. The first program developed back in the 1950s when military officials became concerned about the ability of Air Force staff to manage new technology. The Air Force found a degree program in safety at the University of Southern California that contained some useful courses, and they pumped resources into the program to expand it. Today there are more than twelve thousand systems management graduates from that USC program and its off-shoots. The majority of students now work for civilian rather than military institutions. But the program has not taken hold as one might expect, and it's still largely confined to USC. An effort to expand it several years ago at the University of Denver was unsuccessful.

Recently the University has come up with a **management of technology** program to replace it. The program addresses a related need in high-tech industry to link product design with marketing.

Product life cycles are short in technical fields. In the audio entertainment industry, for example, compact disks overtook cassette tapes and phonograph records in just three years. Soon, digital tapes could replace CDs. Based on that kind of turnover, one might assume that high-tech companies would go all out to hire as many design engineers and inventors as they could. But it seems that speed in creating a new gizmo is not the only factor that determines its success. It's also important for a company to understand from the outset how the product will be manufactured and marketed.

Consider the video cassette recorder. Ampex, the American firm that invented the device, assumed that the VCR would appeal only to broadcasters (much as Edison saw the phonograph record). Sony, on the other hand, foresaw a whole new consumer electronics market. Today, 75 percent of all American homes have VCRs, and Sony dominates the market. That's the power of marketing in high-tech.

Steve Jobs' NeXt computer is another case in point. A co-founder of Apple Computers, Jobs was no novice to the high-tech industry when he founded NeXt. But his interests were primarily technical. He wanted to break new ground by combining the computer with a compact disk player. While that was a powerful inovation, Jobs had failed to keep up with changing consumer tastes. Today most computers are sold with color monitors, but NeXt came only in black and white. Soon after introducing the NeXt computer, Jobs' engineers had to scramble to redesign the product.

In 1987, the U.S. National Research Council issued a report that called for America to train a new breed of technical managers who can make good decisions across the whole spectrum of product development, from design to manufacturing to marketing. The buzz-word for those skills is "concurrent product design." That's an important part of the curriculum in Management of Technology programs across the country. Massachusetts Institute of Technology, Rensselaer Polytechnic Institute, Northwestern University, University of Denver, Case Western Reserve University, and Portland State University all have well-recognized programs. Students are coming to these programs from both technical and nontechnical fields. The first twenty-eight students who enrolled in the University of Denver program were evenly divided. Half had undergraduate degrees in engineering, the other half in business. It's the same pattern we see in health care management and other fields where generalists are being trained to function both in business management and technical areas.

Evaluating New Programs

Those are the kinds of innovations to keep an eye on in graduate business education. There are also many other options. Sometimes they will appear as new directions in MBA programs. Other times they will be an entirely new degree program, such as the MOT. Of course, new degrees always represent a risk. If they're discontinued, graduates will find themselves holding credentials no one else has heard of. On the positive side, most schools and faculty members are likely to devote much more energy to a new program than to an established one. They tend to invest more of themselves in the excitement of a new venture.

The bottom line in choosing any graduate program in business is to look for the connecting points between the worlds of business and academe. Are the faculty who teach in the program in touch with those who are working in their fields? Do they consult with employers and belong to professional associations? Or does the program simply consist of courses that faculty happen to know how to teach? Are they preparing students for traditional corporate management careers in overcrowded specialties such as finance and marketing? If so, one should be careful. This is not a time for courses in business-as-usual.

Finally, it makes sense to consider the growing number of courses offered by professional associations. These groups are constantly in touch with changing skills and jobs in their professions. In the field of systems management, for example, the Institute of Industrial Engineers sponsors self-study courses and an exam that lead to the title Certified Systems Integrator. The program is designed to help industrial engineers broaden their understanding of production and business operations, combining management skills with an understanding of technology.

Industrial engineers are turning up as professional problem-solvers in a number of fields.

The profession began around the turn of the century, as manufacturers attempted to improve the efficiency of their assembly lines. Under the leadership of Frederick Taylor, Henry Ford's right-hand man, industrial engineers used stop watches to perform time and motion studies of assembly-line workers.

Today the engineers still specialize in efficiency, but the factors they measure are more complex. Labor and raw materials now account for only a fraction of production costs. A typical brewery, for example, spends only 5 percent of its budget on beer. Profitability depends on factors such as product design, marketing, and distribution instead.

That's why today's industrial engineers are trained in business as well as mechanical and electrical engineering. Their tools include computer simulations in addition to stop watches. They focus on customizing products while improving cost efficiency.

In the brewing industry, manufacturers must adapt to consumers who prefer to buy beer in 12-pack containers rather than six-packs or cases.

Some of the techniques used by industrial engineers are designed to build teamwork and communication. *Quality function deployment* is a form of matrix analysis that enables producers to weigh customer needs against cost factors at a number of stages as products are designed.

Breakthrough thinking (from the book by the same name by Gerald Nadler and Shozo Hibino), is another popular approach to solving technical and organizational problems. One of its basic principles is to question the purpose of solving a problem before launching in to attach it. The point is to ask "Are we doing the right thing?" before asking "Are we doing things right?"

Recently, when a Wisconsin hospital complained of facing a nursing shortage, industrial engineering consultants determined that the hospital wasn't short of nurses at all. It seemed the nurses they had weren't being utilized properly. The engineers and nurses designed a work-flow system that eliminated information logjams at nursing stations. They put vital information on computers in patients' rooms instead.

That's the kind of innovative approach that has created new demand for industrial engineers. At last report, 30 percent of the Institute of Industrial Engineers' membership was employed in service industries.

The Growing Business of Teaching Business Skills

For those who already have an advanced degree in business—or even some other specialty—there are increasing career opportunities in business education. Some specialists are finding full-time jobs on college business faculties, which is an arena where qualified teachers seem to be in short supply. According to the American Assembly of Collegiate Schools of Business, whereas undergraduate enrollment in the nation's business schools increased 33 percent in the past decade, the ranks of doctoral students have hardly increased at all. Typically, only 3 percent of the PhDs awarded in the United States are in business. Consequently, many schools of business are staffing up with MBAs who have scholarly interests—or who at least enjoy keeping up with current developments in their fields.

Teaching can be a good option for those who already hold an MBA in a specialized field but who find themselves without a corporate employer. Community college teaching is an especially good way for business specialists who enjoy working with people to reconnect with the real world. However, many of the students who are studying business in these schools aren't interested in learning about the corporate world. Often they're business owners who are simply trying to learn enough management skills to survive.

Many schools are coming up with innovative ways to teach entrepreneurs basic business skills, such as using computer spreadsheets. Consider the field of accounting—traditionally a "yawner." New accounting software programs have not only eliminated the tedium of performing hand calculations, they've also invigorated the study of accounting by turning out instant analyses and what-if scenarios from financial data. "What if we change long-distance companies and invest all the money we'll save in a corporate jet? But then, what if the price of fuel goes up?" Three-dimension planners such as Lotus Release 3.0 make these kinds of calculations not only possible but downright fun.

The problem is that many adults who have not grown up with computers are terrified of the machines. Ron Walters, an accounting teacher at the Community College of Aurora, tells me that some people call him several times before they'll enroll in his introductory classes.

"When they finally do sit down at a terminal, you'd swear they were turning on the switch to their own electric chairs," he says. "Later they tell us how easy it is to use computers."

Many mid-life adults find that the logical processes of computers help them grasp basic principles of fields that once mystified them in school. A spreadsheet program can clearly distinguish between fixed and variable costs, for example. But in other instances, computers can spew out so much data that users are overwhelmed. Financial programs are notorious for burying lay people in data.

That's where I've seen another MBA grad find an innovative way to use his training. Chuck Kremer has built a business from creating his own educational program outside of formal schools. Kremer is a CPA and former chief financial officer. Today he concentrates on helping business managers make sense of their financial statements. It's a process that combines skills in accounting, strategic planning, and computer operations.

The One-day MBA

"Research has shown that, even among Fortune 500 managers, 95 percent don't understand how to use their companies' internal financial statements," Kremer says. The problem is that introductory accounting courses focus solely on profit and loss as a single bottom line. In reality, organizations actually have three bottom lines: net income, cash flow, and return on equity. Kremer learned a unique method of correlating those three factors from the late Lou Mobley, a technical executive with IBM who invented his own method of computer-supported accounting out of personal necessity. IBM's traditional financial reports had left him totally confused.

The Mobley Matrix prints out three bottom line columns at the end of each page in a financial statement. Kremer teaches the method in a seminar he calls "The One-day MBA," targeting small-business owners who regularly face make-or-break decisions based on their financial analysis and strategic planning abilities. For example, a business owner may stockpile supplies in order to get a good price—but then run short of operating capital to pay his bills. Or a company may parcel out bonuses to sales representatives on the basis of the contracts their clients sign. They'd be better advised to hold the bonuses until the customers pay for the orders.

For a small business, mistakes of this kind can be disastrous. That's why they need to combine financial management strategies with strategic planning.

"One of the problems with traditional accounting is that it teaches people to manage through a rear-view mirror," Kremer observes. "That may be all right for a corporate manager assigned to collect data for annual reports. But small-business owners need to see the complete picture and make sense of it. They need to manage looking forward."

Kremer is typical of many consultants who are teaching business skills outside traditional business schools.

Applied Management: Teaching the Humanities in the Workplace

But business skills aren't the whole story. Others are teaching all sorts of other subjects in business environments, combining management with specialties as varied as psychology, communication, and the liberal arts. Most of these consultants are career changers with skills from some other discipline. They're not specialists in management.

Here are a half-dozen examples of these new approaches to applied management. As we'll see, in most areas, the skills taught are not intended to produce full-time managers. They're skills to be added to other occupations. For today, management skills must be linked with the ability to do something else.

Some of the most creative management training can be found in short-term, certificate programs for new supervisors who have been promoted up through the ranks. The courses cover topics such as problem-solving and decision-making techniques, interpersonal communication, motivation, negotiation, delegation, management of meetings, conflict management, performance management, managing multiple priorities, and strategic planning.

Here are several typical programs in assertiveness, delegation, and conducting meetings.

Assertiveness for Managers

Lynn Pollard, a management consultant trained in social work, spends much of her time helping managers ask for what they want and say what they mean. She first became interested in the subject of assertiveness back in graduate school, when she worked with impoverished inner-city residents. Many of her clients felt so powerless that they had difficulty even stating their needs to civic officials.

Managers often have similar problems, Pollard believes, especially when they're promoted from within the ranks. It's difficult to establish new relationships with co-workers whom one has known as friends. As a result, she says, supervisors may hide behind rigid policies: "My door is always open" or "My door is always closed."

In dealing with superiors, a non-assertive manager may jeopardize an entire department by failing to speak up for its needs. Pollard once worked with a computer manufacturer whose sales reps spent several months closing a major deal that depended on the customer receiving a customized software package. The manager in charge of software development failed to let his boss know what his staff needed to complete the project. When the time came to deliver the software, it was nowhere to be found.

Pollard believes the same principle applies in the corporate boardroom or the inner city. "Ask for what you need, then see if the environment can support it." In her class with managers, she concentrates on several typical pinch-points for managers: deadlines, delegation, evaluation, and budget control.

"Obviously, I can't reshape my students' personalities in a short course," she acknowledges. "But I can help them anticipate when they're likely to have trouble. They can learn to stop, look, and choose an effective response."

Learning to Delegate

Karen Boringer is a veteran management consultant with another interesting specialty: delegation. Boringer has twelve years' experience as a consultant and a master's degree in organizational communication. But she still remembers an incident early in her career when she learned to pay attention to delegation.

Boringer was working as a secretary, and she'd been put in charge of the office photocopier. Maintaining the Xerox machine was miserable work: clearing jammed paper, changing the messy ink cartridge, and all the rest. But it was her responsibility, and something others needed from her. When she was promoted to office supervisor and told to delegate the copy machine job to someone else, she found that she hated to give it up.

Delegation is like that. It's a process that triggers all sorts of anxiety. What if the person to whom we delegate a task fouls up? Or suppose they're so weighted with other responsibilities that they turn it down? That's typical of downsizing organizations. Employees complain, "Look, we couldn't keep up with this work before, and now we have fewer people to do it." But delegation is crucial to managerial careers. "Learn to delegate, and you can be promoted to higher levels of management," Boringer advises. "Fail to learn, and others will have to delegate work to you." She teaches supervisors to follow three basic guidelines.

✦ Set clear priorities. Learn to separate that which is important from that which is merely urgent. Spend your time on your company's bottom line.

✦ Decide who on your staff is best suited for a given assignment. Usually that's not the supervisor. "It's small comfort to your boss to know that you can outperform your subordinates," she says. "As a manager, you're paid to accomplish work through others."

✦ Create conditions that enable your staff members to succeed. Run through a few steps of an assignment to be sure

they understand it. Establish performance standards and a
system for feedback. Above all, avoid reverse delegation:
"Once the monkey is on someone else's back, don't take it
back on yours."

Building Openness in Organizations

Will Schutz has made a specialty of truth telling. It's the tap-
root skill, he believes, for managing meetings effectively.

Schutz is the psychologist who first gained fame back in the
1960s as a staff member at Esalen. His book *Joy*, which he claims to
have written in a weekend, became a best seller. In recent years he
has tried to adapt some basic principles of encounter groups to business organizations.

The idea is to unhinge the hidden agendas that can sabotage
meetings, or at any rate bog them down. Hidden agendas are tiring,
Schutz says. "When we're not telling the truth, a tremendous
amount of energy goes into that." He believes that work groups can
function more happily and efficiently if supervisors pay attention to
three basic stages in the formation of groups.

+ First there's the question of inclusion. Who is in the group
  and who's not? People will function much more coopera-
  tively if they're assured of belonging.

+ Then there's the matter of control. Who's to lead and who's
  to follow? That's the second item on everyone's agenda.

+ Finally there's openness. How open will members of the
  group be with one another? Schutz believes that if the first
  two phases of group life are resolved, then workers will be
  freed to share their real feelings and agenda. If not, there's
  likely to be a lot of energy expended in the interests of inclusion and control.

Schutz teaches a process of "concordant decision making," in
which everyone affected by a decision has a voice and is encouraged
to speak openly. Asked why he was so quiet, one worker told him, "I
know that at some point you're going to have to ask me. So I don't
have to scream and shout." Schutz acknowledges, however, that
open communication is not every corporate manager's cup of tea. In
an interview published in the *Journal of Counseling and Development*
(March/April, 1992) he said, "So far, I've had just modest success in
terms of making money . . . . What I do is, at the beginning, threat-
ening to some people. In effect I am saying, 'Would you be willing

to tell the truth, and be totally open?'

"Many people tell us directly, 'No, I've spent forty years trying to hide this stuff.'"

He tells the story of a sales representative who continually asked for a raise even though he knew his company couldn't afford it. "Okay, what's your real reason for badgering us?" his bosses finally asked him.

The salesman thought a moment. "I don't think you guys appreciate me," he admitted.

Like many other techniques of applied management, Schutz's principles of truth telling are good for personal growth. Work feels better when people are encouraged to be themselves at the plant or the office. Work becomes an environment where people can grow. That's the way Lynn Pollard views her consulting activities. She said, "I wanted to work with 'well' people, and help them grow. Business seemed like a place to do that."

While selling employers on courses in "soft skills" such as assertiveness training sometimes takes some doing, it's still remarkable to see the range of subjects being taught in the American workplace. Maybe it's because people are trying to meet more of their personal needs on the job. Or perhaps it's because the workplace itself is in such turmoil.

Transition Management

Bill Bridges, a former college English professor, has made a career of helping workers adjust to transitions in companies that are letting lots of people go. Bridges has the air of a caring professor, and his workshops in industry are as comfortable as college lectures. He's fond of quoting passages from history, like this one:

"We trained hard, but every time we were beginning to form up into teams, we would be reorganized. I was to learn later in life that we tend to meet any new situation by reorganizing, and a wonderful method it can be of creating the illusion of progress while producing inefficiency and demoralization." That's from Gaius Petronius, a veteran of the Roman Legion in the First Century A.D.

Bridges believes that many corporate employees today are suffering from the same, two-thousand-year-old complaint. They're victims of organizations in transition. He's trained battalions of part-time counselors to assist workers in methods of managing change.

Honesty in the Workplace

Business ethics is another oddly practical subject. It's a field that has come and gone in American business during the past century. Harvard introduced business ethics courses following the stock market crash of 1929. In recent years, new scandals have rekindled interest in the subject. There was General Dynamics' shenanigans in defense-contracting, the environmental disasters caused by Union Carbide and Exxon, Ivan Boesky's insider trading, and on and on. Today it is increasingly clear that a weak sense of ethics is bad for business.

Whole professions can suffer from moral lapses. The savings and loan debacle of the 1980s is a case in point. When Congress passed the 1982 Garn–St. Germain Act, deregulating the S&L industry, it made all sorts of new investments possible. But that didn't mean they were feasible. The fundamental principles of risk/return ratio remained the same. Some savings and loan officials continued to exercise good professional judgment, regardless of what the law allowed. But others saw an opportunity to make a killing, and they did. They gutted their own profession.

One common response to moral failure is regulation. Tighten the laws. Close all the loopholes. But many business leaders believe that a regulatory environment stifles the initiative of a free economy. They feel the way to improve moral performance is to strengthen the ethical judgment of individuals.

A number of interesting efforts are underway as business schools create new courses in ethics. In 1987 the chairman of the Security and Exchange Commission donated $20 million to the Harvard Business School to develop its ethics curriculum. Corporations are drawing up explicit codes of ethics for employees. Levi Strauss, for example, has stated explicitly that it will not condone its employees' offering bribes to promote business deals, even in countries where that is routinely practiced. Currently more than 90 percent of America's two thousand largest companies have ethical codes of practice.

The Ethics Resource Center of Washington, D.C., offers an excellent series of dramatized video programs on moral dilemmas common to particular professions, from nepotism to industrial spying. It make a particularly good classroom resource. Ethics education is one more subject from the non-business realm of humanities that's gaining value in the changing workplace.

Are there full-time jobs in the field? Not many. But there are opportunities for managers and consultants to pursue ethics education as a part-time occupation.

The same can be said for pursuing other disciplines, such as foreign languages, that can help people become better generalists.

Changing times are good times for those who can teach new skills, especially if they're enterprising enough to create their own classrooms.

The Business-Creation Business: Careers in Economic Development

Finally, let's look at the business of creating jobs for others, from the growing field of economic development. It's one of those fields, like health care management and transportation management, where basic skills in business management may be transferred from one arena to another.

Economic development specialists first appeared in the South about fifty years ago. States like Mississippi and Tennessee set out to diversify their agricultural economies by persuading manufacturers to relocate from the North. They hired economic development promoters to help them. These developers were sometimes known as "smokestack chasers."

In time, the idea of economic development spread to other regions, as states and local communities discovered that they, too, could develop strategies to create new jobs. Often the methods they followed were unsophisticated. Civic officials would designate a cornfield on the outskirts of town as an "industrial park," then hire a retired realtor to beat the bushes for companies interested in relocating. Usually the strategy failed; studies show that only 5 percent of new job growth in the United States comes from corporate relocation.

But in recent years the field of economic development has been growing—in numbers and effectiveness. According to the American Economic Development Council, there now are fifteen thousand development agencies in the United States. Together, they employ eighteen thousand full-time and part-time workers. Those numbers have been growing consistently—perhaps as much as 50 percent to 75 percent just in the past few years.

Development specialists may work for government agencies at the federal, state, or local level; for chambers of commerce; or in public/private partnerships. Recently, most growth has been at the local level in civic and county agencies.

The job responsibilities of development specialists are just as varied. Julie Bender, who directs ECO Aurora, a public/private partnership in suburban Denver, says, "This may be the world's most interdisciplinary field. That's probably why I enjoy it so much." The field seems to be growing in professionalism, too. While it's still possible to find plenty of "reborn realtors" in economic development, most communities are discovering that they need people with solid skills to develop local industries and build employment. Today, several national associations offer training in complex subjects such as economic impact analysis, industry targeting, and business development techniques. Each year the American Economic Development Council sponsors a basic course in economic development at sixteen different sites around the country, plus a three-year series of one-week institutes and a series of executive development seminars.

Another group, The National Development Council, offers courses in economic development finance such as venture capital funding and real estate finance. And a third organization, the National Association of State Development Agencies, sponsors annual conferences on international business at the Thunderbird American Graduate School of International Management in Glendale, Arizona.

How does one go about breaking into the economic development profession? Basically, from the ground up. While advanced skills and certification are becoming more important, economic development is still a who-you-know field. The best strategy is to build entry-level skills as a volunteer with a local chamber of commerce or economic development council—then try to break into a paid staff position, taking courses from AEDC or one of the other national organizations all the while. As in other fields, it makes sense to balance one's skills and experience.

Currently, growth seems to have tailed off. But as the Good Old Boys retire, new opportunities should open up. And as long as there's a need to create new jobs, economic development is one field that seems destined to keep growing.

Resources

Those interested in team-building aspects of management might find two instruments of interest. *"The Personal Relations Survey"* is published by **Teleometrics International**, 1755 Woodstead Court, The Woodlands, Texas 77380. Phone: (713) 367-0060. *"How Is Your Team Working?"* is available from **Organization Design and Development, Inc.**, 2002 Renaissance Boulevard, Suite 100, King of Prussia, Pennsylvania 19406. Phone: (215) 279-2002).

For an overview of programs in business education, the traditional umbrella organization is the **American Assembly of Collegiate Schools of Business**, 605 Old Ballas Road, Suite 220, St. Louis, Missouri 63141.

In an apparent attempt to control the population of MBAs at a time when the numbers of jobs for them were declining, the

AACSB has chosen to accredit only 256 of the 800 MBA programs across the country.

However, in 1989, a second organization was formed to pick up the slack and accredit more of the others. It is the **Association of Collegiate Business Schools and Programs**, ACBSP, based in Overland Park, Kansas. Their accredited programs include more community colleges and second-tier state universities than schools in the academic mainstream. In considering the accreditation of a business school, it's wise to note whether the program is accredited by the AACSB or the ACBSP.

The **American Management Association** sponsors a constant round of publications and conferences on American business. They're at 135 West 50th Street, New York, New York 10020.

The **National Management Association**, which traditionally has focused on middle management issues, 2210 Arbor Blvd., Dayton, Ohio 45439.

For information on the **University of Denver Management of Technology** program, write to University College, University of Denver, Denver, Colorado 80208. The phone number is (303) 871-3968.

The **Institute of Industrial Engineers** is located at 25 Technology Park/Atlanta, Norcross, Georgia 30092. Phone: (404) 449-0460.

Assertiveness for Managers by Diana Cawood is a book Lynn Pollard recommends. It's published by Self-Counsel Press of Canada, at $10.95.

For rental/purchase information about the series, *"Ethics at Work,"* contact the **Ethics Resource Center** at 1120 G. Street, NW, Suite 200, Washington, D.C. 20005. Phone: (202) 737-2258.

Other cases, in print form and mostly on public policy issues, are available from the **John F. Kennedy School of Government** at Harvard University, 79 JFK Street, Cambridge, Massachusetts 02138. Ask for the *Kennedy School Case Catalog.*

For information on training and certification programs in economic development, contact the **American Economic Development Council** at 9801 West Higgins Road, Suite 540, Rosemont, Illinois 60018-4726. Phone: (708) 692-9944.

The **National Development Council** is at 211 East 4th Street, Covington, Kentucky 41011. Phone: (606) 291-0220. The address for the **National Association of State Development Agen-**

cies is 444 North Capital Street, Suite 611, Washington, D.C. 20001. Phone: (202) 898-1302.

AEDC has produced two publications that offer a broad overview of the field: *Economic Development Tomorrow* and *Practicing Economic Development*.

Chapter Ten

Consulting: Skills and Options

This chapter looks at the skills required to establish a successful consulting practice, and considers some new kinds of organizations and workstyles for consultants and other independent practictioners.

These formats include outsourcing firms that employ former corporate workers, in-house consultants, and cooperatives for independent consultants: all innovative ways to work in today's entrepreneurial economy.

✦   ✦   ✦

Add the numbers, and it's hard to find a field that's growing as fast as consulting. At last count there were 450,000 consultants in the United States, and they were multiplying at the rate of 16 percent a year.

A profitable growth industry—right?

Not necessarily. For many people who have left corporate careers involuntarily, "consulting" is nothing but a polite way to spell UNEMPLOYMENT. There's nothing necessarily profitable about hanging out a shingle as a consultant.

But with good skills and careful planning, many mid-career professionals have established profitable consulting practices that have continued for the rest of their lives. Others have filled what might have been wasted time, meeting expenses while building bridges to new employers. In either case, serving a tour of duty as a consultant can be a worthwhile career move, if it's a strategy based on careful planning.

As one who has done a couple of stints in consulting, I've found that it's helpful to follow a three-step process when deciding whether to set up a practice. It's a simple process based on three questions: What, Who, and How? This is the way I approach those questions.

WHAT

What is it that you have to market as a consultant? Have you developed some sort of special expertise in the course of your career? Try to identify some of your distinctive services or products.

Here's a good way to begin. Do a bit of "reverse engineering" on your work history, like the industrial spies who disassemble a product in order to discover what makes it tick. Draw a couple of lines down a sheet of paper, creating three columns. Head the first column TASKS, the second SKILLS, and the third TRAITS. Then, for each job you've held, imagine that you're hiring someone to take your place. Analyze the job, one column at a time. What tasks would your successor have to perform in order to succeed you? What skills would be required to accomplish those tasks? What traits, such as assertiveness or self-direction, would be required to use the skills effectively?

You will find specific examples of this technique in the appendix.

While this is not a complicated procedure, it takes time to do well. As in any kind of personal reflection, it's important to work at the process in increments, a bit at a time, in a quiet place where you can relax. Reading the material aloud to someone who knows you well often helps fill in the gaps of material you might overlook.

Remember that self-analysis is always a challenging, paradoxical process. Although you know yourself better than anyone else, you're also too close to your own experience to have much perspective on it. As the old saying goes, "Whoever it was who discovered water, it probably wasn't a fish." So in completing the process, don't rush it.

It's important to analyze volunteer assignments as well as paid jobs. Last year I worked with an aerospace engineer who was giving serious thought to a change of direction. He decided to do this analysis on a particularly challenging experience he'd had as a volunteer, when his church had asked him to coordinate the process of firing their minister.

The engineer had drawn on an array of skills in conflict resolution and organizational development, subjects he'd studied in seminars at work but had never fully used there. By isolating the skills as he wrote them down on paper, the engineer could see them more clearly.

He gave serious thought to whether he wanted to work in the field of organizational communication within technical fields, an arena where many engineers feel there's a great deal of work to be done. Which leads to the next question: Who?

WHO

Who is willing to pay for and otherwise support the work you believe needs doing? Who's buying what you're selling? That's the point at which many consulting careers flounder, when people fail to consider the market demand for what they can do. If we're going to be successful selling specialized skills, we must take time to determine that we have a market.

Sometimes the best client for a consultant's services is his or her former employer. An individual who has learned about the problems of a particular organization by working there may be in a strong position to treat its ills. The test is whether one's ex-employer sees the relationship that way. It's the old marketing distinction between perceived needs and felt needs. Does the ex-employer see the need? Who's buying?

That brings us to a new trend in consulting that has special significance for ex-corporate employees: "Outsourcing." Outsourcing is when a company hires independent consultants instead of in-house staff. It's increasingly common in corporations that have released large numbers of professional workers. Again, some of the independents are former employees. Outsourcing can be a lucrative source of contracts, at least for a time. But depending, as an independent contractor, on a single Sugar Daddy for consulting business does not make for feelings of career security.

During the past several years there has been a mounting increase in the ranks of companies providing outsourced services. The practice has been especially popular in data services, where analysts have found outsourcing growing at 40 percent a year. What was a $4.6 billion industry in 1989 is projected to reach $38 billion by 1995.

Rick Reid, a former data processing manager for a large discount merchandiser, currently serves as vice president for American Management Systems, a computer operations company that lives off outsourcing. AMS has 3,600 employees, which is twice the number it had five years ago.

Reid has seen outsourcing from both inside and out. He was a manager at a company whose staff members were laid off when the work of their department was outsourced. Now, as an officer of AMS, he's actively involved in hiring former corporate employees. Over the years, Reid has found that while outsourcing may eliminate jobs, it also can open new opportunities. That's because outsourcing firms are often prospective full-time employers. Moreover, many workers have found that by signing on with a company that specializes in their profession, they receive much better training and mentoring than they would by working for an employer who's in a different business. In corporate law, for example—a growing arena for outsourcing—an isolated in-house lawyer may find a better professional environment with a law firm that deals in outsourced corporate business. The same may be true in data processing, where an activity that's peripheral to one business may be central to another.

One of the latest trends in outsourcing is employee leasing, wherein companies turn over all their in-house human resource management functions to an outside firm that acts as employer-of-record. The movement has been growing phenomenally (at least 30 percent a year). Currently, there are one million leased employees in the United States, officially "employed" by more than thirteen hundred leasing companies.

For small companies, the chief motive for outsourcing personnel functions is usually to negotiate better health insurance rates by combining one's own employees with those of other employers. But, as in other fields, there's growing emphasis on employing specialists that small companies couldn't afford. Recently I visited an HR outsource firm whose staff includes a full-time labor attorney, a specialist in risk management and safety, an authority on insurance, and a psychologist who works in training and leadership development.

Outsourcing may be an attractive alternative to independent consulting. Ex-corporate employees who find work with outsource-contract firms may avoid having to rely on their own resources for all the management skills required. Which leads to the third question for prospective consultants: HOW?

HOW

How will you manage your practice? Consulting is like any small business, in the range of skills required. There's the business of drumming up business, to begin with. Paul and Sarah Edwards, authors of *The Best Home Businesses for the 90s*, estimate that 40 percent of the time required to manage a business is spent selling one's services. Not everyone takes to that kind of self-promotion.

Contract negotiation is another crucial skill. While some large organizations may have boiler-plate contracts on hand and in-house attorneys to do the negotiation, others will look to consultants to frame their own deals. Even when a company does offer a structured contract, sometimes it calls for revision. A friend of mine was offered a consulting assignment by a large corporation that happened to be his ex-employer. They wanted him to work on a special project with a new division in another city. While the contract they offered provided employment only for the duration of the assignment, there was a possibility that it could turn into a new full-time job. The assignment was an opportunity to showcase his talents.

But when my friend took a look at the project, he found that it was poorly designed. Not only did it fail to address the real work that needed to be done, but it could be completed in no time at all. So he proposed a different kind of arrangement, in which he'd be paid for a block of his time. That way he'd have some income he could count on and could do a good job on the assignment.

The revision worked. The project was a success, and my friend was offered another full-time position.

Some of the negotiation skills necessary for outside consultants may also be useful to those who work in corporations. Joseph Hanson, an analyst of technical careers, finds that many engineers who once served as narrowly defined technical specialists now find themselves involved in a constant round of ad-hoc projects where working relationships are constantly changing. Hanson calls them "in-house consultants."

Like any consultants, he says, in-house consultants should pay attention to the stages of the relationships they form with clients. A consulting project, as he describes it, is almost like a romance. First there is a period of anxious fears during the initial client contact. Then comes the clarifying of expectations, followed by a time when clients and consultants take stock of the relationship. Finally the relationship is brought to a close, perhaps to be renewed in another project when the cycle will be repeated.

One other feature of the How question is vitally important to independent consultants. That's the issue of how one feels about working alone. It's one thing to be in business *for* yourself, but being in business *by* yourself may be another matter.

Steve Hinds, a human resource management consultant, may have found a way out of the dilemma. Hinds has formed a loose cooperative with a half-dozen other consultants. Each is a specialist in a different facet of personnel management: corporate training, compensation and benefits, recruiting, and the like. The group gets together about once a month to discuss professional concerns and to share referrals. That's all the structure they have at this point. There are no bylaws and no regular meeting place. The group doesn't even have a name.

But Hinds has a vision for its future. He intends to keep the network small and carefully screened, with only one specialist per field. Each member of the group will be someone he knows and trusts, someone he can refer to a client with confidence. Already the group is considering publishing a brochure on their various services and sharing a suite of offices.

The consulting cooperative is an interesting concept. As America reorganizes as a nation of entrepreneurs, groups like this may become more common. Consultant cooperatives would be a natural market for commercial real estate firms, for example, as they rent executive office suites. Instead of letting suites to entrepreneurs who have nothing in common but the need for a receptionist and a copy machine, why not recruit a synergistic group of specialists in the same field?

Like outsourcing and in-house consulting, it's an idea that seems made for the times.

Resources

For an in-depth view of managing a consulting practice, look for the books and tapes of Howard Shenson. His book *Contract and Fee-Setting Guide for Consultants and Professionals* sells for $19.95.

Todd G. Buchholz' book, *New Ideas from Dead Economists: An Introduction to Modern Economic Thought*, is published by New American Library, a division of Penguin Books.

Paul and Sarah Edwards' *The Best Home Businesses for the 90s* is published by Jeremy P. Tarcher Press for $10.95.

Joseph Hanson's article, "Effective Engineers Are Internal Consultants," is available from the Novations Group in Provo, Utah. Phone: (801) 375-7525.

Chapter Eleven

Health Care

This chapter addresses one of the fastest-growing industries in history. Today, the need for health care workers is growing out of sight.

Yet the field deserves careful scrutiny, because of many unanswered questions about paying for the kinds of services health care professionals provide. We'll consider several health care careers, and some of those questions, at length.

If jobs grew directly from demand, health care would seem to be the career of the century. Just look at the statistics. In the United States, health care already totals 13 percent of the Gross National Product. And that's just for starters. According to the U.S. Department of Commerce, "Expenditures on health care are expected to rise 11 percent, from an estimated $738 billion in 1991 to $817 billion in 1992, and to increase at an average annual rate of 12 to 13 percent during the next five years."

No wonder the U.S. Department of Labor advises, "Some of the best job prospects during the next decade will be in health care . . . health-related occupations will account for about one of eight new jobs by the year 2000."

The predictions are more than promising, as far as they go. But now for the bad news.

Job growth depends upon factors other than demand, regardless of what the government labor economists say. There's also the matter of resources. As consumers, we must find a way to pay for what we want. That's where the rosy outlook in health care jobs begins to fade.

The bottom-line question in health care is simply this: who

will pay the bill?

That question has been mounting in the United States as health care costs doubled during the past decade. Prescription expenses went up 152 percent and hospital costs doubled *within the past two years alone.*

Part of the expense Americans are paying has nothing to do with medical services. It's the cost of medical malpractice insurance, fed by lawsuits filed by America's hordes of lawyers. Malpractice claims increased by one-third in the early 1980s. During the entire decade of the eighties, malpractice insurance premiums went up 18 percent per year.

According to the U.S. Department of Commerce, the rising tide of litigation has given rise to a great deal of redundant testing intended to safeguard physicians against lawsuits. Some estimate that "defensive medicine" adds 15 billion dollars a year to the nation's health care bill.

The outlook in health care occupations, then, will clearly depend upon factors other than an increasing demand for health services. For the foreseeable future, employment in the health care industry will be pushed and pulled by three forces: demographics, technology, and financing.

The demographic facts in health care are simply stated. America's population is out of balance. The nation has an enormous, swollen generation of Baby Boomers in its middle. One-third of our population was born in an eighteen-year period just after World War II. For health care professionals, that Baby Boom cohort is very significant. The Boomers are marching through mid-life toward the last, aging stages of maturity, followed by a birth-dearth of younger Americans who are in no shape, statistically, to fund the Baby Boomers' Social Security programs. Sooner or later the financial crunch is coming.

Of course, the funding questions are turning up already. Plenty of analysts have noted that the United States, while paying half again as much for health care as Canada, has 37 million citizens without insurance. It's also apparent that Medicare costs are mounting, as Americans continue to live longer. Last year, in fact, the costs increased four times faster than the number of clients served.

The point is that anyone who's considering a career in one of the health care occupations must be prepared to work in a constantly changing environment where skills in management and cost containment may be just as important as methods of treatment. Those factors are already clear in many of today's changing health care fields. Let's review job prospects in several of these fields, as they're evolving.

When we think of jobs in the health care field, most of us focus on a few traditional roles: physician, nurse, physical therapist. In fact, however, health care comprises an array of job titles.

Recently I moderated a panel discussion that included the president of a large hospital in Denver. As he got up to speak, I noticed that he was holding a thick computer printout (I hoped it was not his speech). It turned out to be a list of job titles within his institution. Holding the printout at shoulder height, he unfurled it till it reached the floor. There were 240 titles in all: everything from gift shop manager to critical-care nurse to something called "cast technician." That's a person who specializes in setting broken limbs.

One of the challenges in hospital management today is working with all those constituencies. A hospital is a sort of consortium of craft guilds. Almost every specialty that's been around for a few years has an association of its own, with a good-sized political agenda. That's why there's so much politicking among them. In recent years, two of the most active political groups have been physicians and nurses. Their conflicts stem not only from health care but from politics in the larger culture.

Nursing

Time was when the relationship between doctor and nurse was a clear-cut hierarchy. A middle-aged friend of mine in nursing describes her early training in the field. "Back in the fifties, you knew your status," she said. "If you were sitting in the nurses' station and a doc walked in, you got up and gave him your chair. If you were writing on a chart, you handed him your pen as well."

The women's movement challenged many of those practices. So did the shortage of nurses that emerged in the 1980s. Enrollment in nursing schools plummeted 27 percent during one three-year period in the mid-eighties, as nurses complained about inadequate pay scales. Many women began to turn to medicine instead.

Meanwhile, the demand for nurses grew. Between 1972 and 1986, hospitals doubled the number of nurses assigned per patient. Soon, 80 percent of all qualified nurses in the U.S. were working, and 99 of every 100 new registered nurses found employment. And still there were not enough nurses, as one in ten hospital nursing positions stood vacant. In large urban hospitals, families hired private nurses through temporary employment agencies. The temps provided post-operative care for patients who found that when they rang the bell for a nurse, no one responded.

As shortages mounted in the late 1980s, a full-scale confrontation between nurses and physicians ensued. The American Medical Association devised a plan to remedy the shortage of nurses not by raising their pay or improving their working conditions, but by replacing them with paraprofessional workers. They concocted a new job title, the "registered care technician." RCTs were to be a kind of health aide who would be trained and supervised by nurses. Paid at minimum wage, the RCTs would end the labor shortage and reduce costs in the bargain.

. As it happened, the AMA proposal never got off the ground. Nurses organized, rallying to protest through their professional associations. Attendance at annual nursing conventions tripled as the nurses mounted a powerful lobbying movement to defeat the RCT proposal. It was the kind of effort that would have been impossible before the women's movement.

Today the tide has turned. Nurses are not only enjoying rising salaries and status, in some quarters they are also challenging the top-dog hegemony of physicians. Some maintain that nurses, rather than doctors, should become the primary care providers, since they are the experts in bedside care. American medicine is overrun by high-tech specialties, they say, with experts and devices for everything under the sun. What's needed is a specialist in coordinating the specialties—an ombudsman and manager of patient care.

Their candidate for this position is, of course, the nurse. In a move to upgrade their status and promote the new role, several schools have established doctoral programs in nursing. It's a political move as much as academic—an effort to match the physicians' hallowed title of "doctor."

Meanwhile, amidst all the politicking, here is how the field looks for now. Nursing professionals come in two basic categories: licensed practical nurses and registered nurses. LPNs, who receive twelve to fourteen months of post-high-school training, are the smaller group, and their numbers are diminishing. Registered nurses, the dominant group, study anywhere from two to four years before taking state board exams. Salaries and working conditions vary widely. In the late 1980s, the average annual salary for RNs was $21,000, with an average maximum of $32,160.

Therein lies a problem. In most fields, professional salaries increase 100 to 200 percent over time. But nurses salaries top out within their first ten years. For now, no immediate solution presents itself. In a profession where some people have degrees and some do not, levels of training vary widely across the United States. Nation-wide, only 20 percent of all hospital nurses are college graduates.

In time it is likely that nursing education will become more standardized. But currently the profession is spinning off all sorts of new advanced-degree programs, without much coordination. For in-stance, there are programs of study for physicians' assistants (who work under the supervision of physicians) and programs for nurse practitioners (for those who prefer a more independent work style). Doctor of Nursing studies run the gamut in quality and subject mat-ter. Some programs provide rigorous training in PhD-caliber re-search; others offer strange series of humanities courses ("Caring in the History of Western Civilization," "Caring in the Arts," etc.).

One of the most fertile fields for RNs may turn out to be ad-vanced medical technology. Remember the high-tech hospital back in chapter 3, with fifteen new treatment technologies in the past year and a PhD and a high school grad filling the same job? The ad-ministrator of that hospital is a proponent of hiring nurses because of their basic undergraduate education in the sciences. He believes that many nurses may find themselves shifting from specialty to specialty throughout the course of their careers, and that they'll be highly marketable because they're readily retrainable.

I shared that idea with a veteran career counselor, who ob-jected vigorously. "Do you really think students go into nursing in order to operate machines?" she asked. "Nursing is a caring profes-sion. Those people are looking for the kinds of relationships that come with long-term patient care. They're not going to be content running machines."

However the hospital drama of nurses and physicians finally unfolds, it's clear that the final scene hasn't yet been written. But there are other intriguing stories evolving outside the hospital envi-ronment. One of them is the birth of a new institution for the dying: the hospice.

Hospice Management

In 1976, Caroline Jaffe read a newspaper notice about a forthcoming lecture on the hospice movement. A registered nurse, Jaffe had heard a bit about St. Christopher's, a new British institution to pro-vide support for terminally ill patients and their families. She called up another nurse friend and a couple of cancer patients and invited them all to attend.

The story of St. Christopher's fascinated her. So the following year, with a small grant from the American Cancer Society, Jaffe founded a hospice of her own. Within a month it had five patients. In 1990, fourteen years after the lecture, the organization had eighty-two employees and a budget of $2.5 million.

Hospices are one of the fastest-growing institutions in the United States. Today, less than twenty years after the founding of St. Christopher's, there are fourteen hundred hospices across the country with twelve thousand salaried employees and another eighty thousand volunteers. Hospices are a bigger growth industry than video rental stores.

But the rampant growth has brought new challenges. Managing hospices has become a big business, especially since 1983, when they became eligible for Medicare funding. That's because of new federal initiatives in medical record keeping.

In the early 1980s, when the federal government faced health care expenditures that were growing at twice the rate of the Gross National Product, officials instituted a new system of accounting regulations that required exacting reports. The new program was an administrative tradeoff. Hospices could garner several thousand dollars in grant support for each of their eligible patients, provided they could cope with the reports. Unfortunately, many couldn't. Today only one hospice in three has developed the financial management skills necessary to qualify for Medicare funding.

The new challenge is reshaping the workforce in hospices. Some feel there's a growing need for another professional role: specially trained financial officers who can deal with the federal bureaucracy. Meanwhile, nurses continue to provide most patient care, and physicians have moved into more of the managerial roles. Social workers have taken over many counseling functions.

Many health care professionals find themselves wrestling with career/value decisions. Should one serve as a technical specialist or a caregiver? Caroline Jaffe recently resigned as director of the hospice she founded. She's returned to caring for dying patients.

I asked Jay Mahoney, president of the National Hospice Organization, about the changing patterns of occupations. He got his start in the field as a staff member in Jaffe's hospice.

"There's no denying our work is changing," Mahoney said. "Nowadays we need both health care providers and health care managers. We'll continue to need that blend of skills as hospices grow. But we can't forget the skills that got us to this point. It was not that we were skilled reimbursement specialists who could manage Medicare. We've succeeded because of the quality of our care."

Managing Health Care Practices

Have MBA: Will travel.

Some managers who have lost corporate jobs are finding new life in health care administration. The field is mushrooming, according to the Medical Group Management Association, a professional association for health care administrators and physicians. MGMA has a membership of 18,500 organizations and individuals across the country. For the past fifteen years, their numbers have doubled every five years. That's an indication of how fast the business of managing health care is growing.

According to Fred Graham, associate director of MGMA, health care administration is a good field for career changers. "It's a field you find by accident," he says. "I don't know of anybody who grows up wanting to be a group practice administrator."

There are three typical career paths in the field. Some people work their way up from a clerical position to office manager and then into some more specialized management job, usually while taking courses after hours. A second path is to earn an MHA—a Master of Health Administration degree—through one of fifty graduate programs in health care administration around the country.

While MHA programs originally focused on hospital administration, most schools have revised their courses to cover new health care delivery systems such as health maintenance organizations. When considering an MHA degree, however, it's important to note that the numbers of schools offering this degree are not growing. According to Graham, that's because many hospitals prefer to hire managers from other industries in order to get fresh perspectives on problems such as quality control and customer service. "The best candidate for a quality assurance position in a hospital may not be someone from another hospital," says Graham. "It's probably some manager of quality control in a theme park or an airline, where customer service is a top priority."

So career path number three is to transfer skills, and perhaps MBA training in business operations, into health care administration. MGMA has established a placement service for people seeking entry to the field, as well as a career assessment program for those already in health care adminstration who find that their jobs are changing and that they may need to consider new directions.

The association also sponsors continuing-education courses to help members update their skills. One of the current up-and-coming skills is Outcomes Measurement: evaluating the cost and success rates of alternative courses of treatment in order to satisfy insurance companies and other third-party payers.

Courses in business are popular among health care administrators, as well. A recent MGMA program at Northwestern University featured seminars on financial analysis, business development plans, leadership styles and team building, and negotiation/conflict resolution. Half the students enrolled in the seminars were physicians. "We're trying to involve administrators and doctors in the same courses," says Graham. "It's a way to help them develop some shared concepts and a common language about business problems."

Allied Health Care Managers

Training managers is a constant challenge in allied health care: second-line professions such as laboratory technology that support the work of physicians and nurses. Some colleges and universities have established special programs to help technically trained workers learn the finer points of management.

Joe Miles, at age thirty-eight, was a typical student when I interviewed him at the University of Denver in 1990. A biology major in college, he'd switched to medical technology because of its promising employment prospects. Today he has established a solid career as a hospital laboratory-services director. But he's learned the profession largely by the seat of his pants.

The program in health care administration Miles completed at the University of Denver offers a broad range of courses in everything from fiscal management to writing proposals. The university recruits students like Miles (those in mid-career), and helps them form a strong support group. In addition, they've hired instructors who not only have graduate training in health care but who also serve as practitioners in the field.

Dan Stenersen, one of the professors, is a nursing home administrator who enjoys the challenge of teaching students with a good base of technical skills but only a faint grasp of larger health care systems. Stenersen says, "We live in a society without a coherent health care policy. That poses new problems every day. To function as managers, our students need solid problem-solving skills. Not just filling out forms; they're good at that. It's when they encounter a problem beyond their formulary thinking that they're stumped. Most of them need alternative ways to frame problems and search for solutions."

For some health care professionals, that translates to a three-sided perspective—the ability to view a problem in health care delivery from the viewpoints of *patient*, *provider*, and *payer*. It's the kind of management training that is probably most effective with experienced practitioners in mid-career.

If managing health care services offers rising job opportunities, delivering the services presents constant challenges. In health care, the jobs require more than training. Personal values and qualities of character such as courage and caring are vitally important as well. As the old adage goes, "Don't go into health care if you don't care."

Respiratory Therapy

Respiratory therapy is an especially challenging field. The profession has been around for some time, but it's been growing in recent years due to advances in home oxygen systems and increasing numbers of patients. Some attribute the patient growth to the popularity of smoking during World War II. Young adults who took up the habit then are suffering pulmonary consequences today.

Helen Jones, who directs a respiratory therapy training program in a vocational school, discovered the respiratory field by accident. She was a licensed practical nurse working in a rural hospital in Nebraska, not far from an interstate highway. During off-hours when there wasn't much to do (which was much of the time), Jones amused herself by learning to operate new equipment in the emergency room.

One night she was fiddling with a new respirator when the emergency room doors flew open and a team of paramedics brought in a truck driver who had crashed into a bridge abutment head-on. The doctor on call was struggling to save the driver when he remembered having seen Jones working with the respirator. "Revive him!" he told her. "Put a tube down his throat!"

"Hell, I can't even find his face," she hollered.

Years later she still remembers the trauma of that experience, but also the sense of feeling needed.

Frustrated and underemployed as an LPN, Jones found respiratory work gratifying. It was something people needed that she could do, and a path toward personal growth. She went on to complete a degree in the field and ultimately became a teacher. The program she directs trains professionals at two levels. Certified respiratory therapy technicians train for twelve months, registered respiratory therapists for twenty-four. Each curriculum requires field experience beginning in the second term. Even the one-year program calls for 720 hours of direct patient contact. That's to ensure that students understand the realities of working with terminal patients and life-threatening illness.

Jones observes, "People are living through the effects of smoking . . . barely. Some of our patients have no lungs or only parts of lungs. They're dying slowly by centimeters, not even by inches."

She adds, "Emphysema is the worst disease I've ever seen."

Her trainees take classes in cardiopulmonary physiology, pharmacology, and oxygen therapy technology, and seminars on death and dying and self-protection from AIDS. Graduates of both twelve- and twenty-four-month programs sit for the same national exam, and they're paid comparable salaries, from $24,000 to $26,000 for those with one year's experience. Top professionals may earn $50,000 annually.

As in other health care professions, there's a constant need to update skills. When Jones entered the field in 1978, there were three basic respiratory medications; today there are thirty.

Dentists and Their Co-workers

In all the churning labor market, there is probably no occupation with more ups and downs than dentistry. The turbulence began in the 1940s, with the introduction of fluoride to water supplies in America. An uncertain experiment to reduce tooth decay, in time the program proved phenomenally successful. Today, one-half of all school children have never had a cavity, and the percentage is still falling.

But in the 1970s, before the effectiveness of fluoride had been established, U.S. health officials became worried that the nation could run short of dentists. They established a "capitation" program to reward schools of dentistry according to their numbers of graduates. Not surprisingly, the numbers soared. Dentists increased at twice the rate of the population. In Texas alone, three schools turned out 1,200 dentists a year. Baby Boomers flocked to the field as they reached grad-school age. It was a good growth profession—except for the success of fluoride.

Soon after the floodtide of dentistry school enrollments, the income of dentists began to fall by 5 percent a year. In the last decade, many dentists have struggled to eke out a living, while others have left the field altogether. Meanwhile the expense of maintaining a practice has continued to rise in cost, not only for equipment and staff, but also for malpractice insurance.

Not long ago my dentist handed me this clipping from an advice column in a professional dentistry journal. The column was headed, "Dentists and the Law."

Question: "Following periodontal surgery, I prophylactically prescribed Ampicillin. When the patient became pregnant shortly after surgery, she sued me on behalf of her newborn. I understand from her friends that the newborn is healthy. How can I be liable for a newborn without any paternity claim?"

The columnist's response was not encouraging. He indicated that the dentist might indeed be liable for child support, right through college expenses.

Today the profession seems to be concentrating on two new arenas for treatment: meeting the needs of an aging population and preventive dentistry. Aging Americans are a major market, as more people keep their teeth. During a recent sixteen-year period, the numbers of individuals who had lost all of their teeth declined by 20 percent. There are promising new techniques in dental implants and bone regeneration for those who wear dentures. But the real opportunity is in preventive dental care. A recent task force report on prevention lists a hundred different techniques for maintaining teeth through hygiene.

The occupational roster in dentists' offices looks like this. At the top, there are dentists who study for eight years, followed by hygienists who train for two to four, then dental assistants who study one or two years (certified dental assistants and expanded functions assistants, respectively), and dental aides who train for six months.

For the last several years, all of the allied health professions have experienced falling numbers—for a variety of reasons. One factor is the declining number of young adults: the birth dearth since the Baby Boom. But there's more to the shortage than that, beginning with the notion of an "allied health profession" itself.

Health care professions have been notoriously hierarchical. Remember the nurse who was taught to give up her chair and pencil when a physician walked in? The hierarchies have been gender-biased, which is to say that, traditionally, most physicians and dentists were male, most "allied" workers female. As already noted, this pattern has changed radically with the women's movement of the last couple of decades. Currently, one-half of medical school students are female, as are one-third of dentistry students. Surveys consistently show more young women favoring a career in medicine than in nursing. Polls of female college freshmen report a 300-percent increase in the number of young women interested in business careers, and a 50-percent decline of interest in nursing.

Women have been breaking down the bastions of male-dominated professions and prospering once they entered the new fields. Recently I heard a hospital administrator report that the practices of women health professionals are increasing at three times those of men, across the board.

That's one explanation for the shortage of allied health professionals: the women's movement. But there are others. Males have failed to take up the slack, for one thing. Just as the numbers of male nurses have held at a constant three percent while females left the field for medicine, so has it been with dentistry. When was the last time you had your teeth cleaned by a male dental assistant?

Americans still suffer from the strictures of an outmoded, lingering class consciousness. Dentists and doctors are seen as full-fledged white-collar professionals—regardless of market conditions. Upwardly mobile young people flock to these prestigious professions. And yet there are excellent opportunities in what we used to think of as "allied health" or "paraprofessions."

Take dental assistants. The occupation dates from the nineteenth century, when female assistants were employed by dentists to dust furniture and to chaperone. In the 1960s the work changed radically with advances in technology. "Four-handed" dentistry became the norm, as the time required to cement a crown was reduced from one hour to two minutes. A good assistant, it was determined, could increase the revenue from a dental practice by 75 percent.

Because of social attitudes, however, pay scales and job status have risen only grudgingly, meaning that not even market demand has been able to stimulate sufficient supplies of new workers. A 1988 American Dental Association survey of dental practices found that 28 percent of dentists had an opening for a hygienist, and 31 percent for an assistant. One dentist in Connecticut was forced to hire a hygienist through a temporary employment service. Salary: $33 an hour. Meanwhile, the number of graduates from dental assistant programs has dropped precipitously, from 6,600 in 1978 to 4,600 in 1987. Dental hygiene grads fell from 5,000 to 3,800 during the same nine-year period. Even the numbers of training programs declined.

The old hierarchical system based on undervalued female labor is crumbling. Those who can look beyond it will recognize that many of the best new jobs in today's market are for "technoprofessionals"—skilled service providers who can manage sophisticated technology and aren't afraid to work with their hands. Most of those jobs pay good wages in a clean environment. Salaries for dental hygienists in Colorado range upward of $30,000 a year.

The drama of dentistry features most of the factors that have influenced today's labor market, from revolutionary technology to reorganized labor force and a changing clientele. The profession is, in many ways, a parable of our time.

Now let's look at some of the new jobs and training opportunities that are appearing in two other rapidly evolving health-related fields.

Biotechnology

Mention "biotechnology" and most people look blank. Sure, they've heard all sorts of growth projections: how the biotech industry could expand as much as 50 percent a year and overtake electronics. But where are the jobs in biotechnology really? Is there any substance to the field?

Eric Dunlop, Professor of Chemical Engineering at Colorado State University, has heard those questions repeatedly. A native of Glasgow, Scotland, he spent seven years in biotech research with the large British pharmaceutical company ICI before coming to the United States. In all, he's been working in biotechnology for seventeen years. "For a long time people asked, 'Is this for real?'" he recalls. "In fact, there were times when I wondered, too!"

Today the industry is very much alive, as biotech companies begin to gear up for production. One such company, Synergen, has been hiring an average of one person a day. The reason the industry is growing is not just that it is producing new products. It's also that biotechnology is producing familiar products in more efficient ways. According to Dunlop, many common pain killers are derived solely from the opium poppy—from which other, infamous narcotics are made. In the past, any effort to boost production of poppies for pain killers increased the stock of illegal narcotics as well. Now, however, the necessary opiates can be produced in the laboratory. The new technology can also create substitutes for rare plants such as the Madagascar periwinkle, source of an anti-leukemia drug, and the Pacific yew tree, from which the cancer drug Taxol is produced. Currently it takes the bark of two yew trees to produce enough Taxol to treat one cancer patient, and two hundred years to grow one tree.

Dunlop is director of a new bioprocessing center in Fort Collins, Colorado, that provides technical support to start-up ventures and training for companies that are preparing to start production. Bioprocessing, the basic technology of biotech jobs, involves growing living cells to create a desired compound—usually a pharmaceutical product or a foodstuff. The process has two phases. *Fermentation* is the process of growing the desired cells in a large vat designed to keep other organisms out. "It's a matter of producing what you want while keeping the nasties out, and making sure your product doesn't grow all over the environment," says Dunlop. That business of keeping the product contained is known as "biosafety." It's a developing specialty in its own right.

The second component of bioprocessing is *bioseparation*. That's extracting the desired substance from its cellular material and surrounding fluids.

Technicians in both fermentation and bioseparation need some knowledge of biology, botany, biochemistry, and microbiology, according to Dunlop. "You're dealing with very sensitive biological material that has its own characteristics. And the more mathematically literate you are, the better off you are," he adds.

That's not to say that everyone in the field has that sort of training. Many people without college training have learned to be biotechnicians on the job. But today is a new era in biotechnology, as more firms begin production; formal training is becoming more vital.

Dunlop offers graduate courses in fermentation and bioseparation for individuals with a college degree in a technical field. The courses provide an entry to managerial as well as technical careers in biotechnology. They're also useful for financial specialists such as venture capitalists, who raise funds to support research in the field. Dunlop's work is one more example of bridging skills across disciplines, to build dialogue within small organizations in high-tech fields.

Environmental Health

Another major frontier field in health is emerging from several different disciplines. Currently, there are only twenty-three accredited programs in environmental health across the country, and most of them are very new. When it comes to employment, however, the track record of environmental health is unmistakable. Environmental health graduates are getting jobs.

The field comprises three basic subjects: industrial hygiene, environmental toxicology, and epidemiology. Undergraduates take a broad range of courses in all three subjects; graduate students specialize in one of the three. The jobs they enter tend to be staff positions in industry or government, where there's a need for a broad range of competencies in hazardous materials management and pollution control. (Unlike environmental consulting, covered in chapter 15, "Teaching and Updating Technical Skills," environmental health is a field for generalists.)

While jobs are growing steadily, they're not always easy to locate, for they go by different names. In the 1930s and 40s, there was an effort to standardize the professional title: sanitarian.

But the title didn't take. Last year, when the National Environmental Health Association surveyed its 5,700 members, they found 298 different job titles, everything from Air Sampling Technicians to Food Protection Manager to Water Quality Planner. It's a reminder of how quickly job titles come and go, and that it's not what we're called but what we do that has staying power.

Environmental health has gone through several revolutions since the nineteenth century, when scientists first established a connection between cholera and dirty water. As time went on, other kinds of bacteria were linked to other diseases such as tuberculosis.

In the 1960s, the environmental field shifted once again. Rachel Carson's book, *Silent Spring*, argued that environmental problems went deeper than bacteria. Carson showed that pesticides were poisoning many species of life, and the environmental movement was born.

Today, while progress has been made in reducing some pollutants such as auto emissions, new problems are emerging. The move to conserve energy by sealing office buildings has triggered illnesses caused by indoor air (which is ten times more polluted than the outdoor variety).

Add to that the hazards of radon (the second leading cause of lung cancer) and lead-contaminated water, and it's clear why the field of environmental health is growing.

Currently, most jobs are found in government agencies such as county health departments and in engineering consulting firms. But other jobs could emerge in far-flung fields such as banking. Eventually, environmental testing may be required for mortgage approval.

In addition to the people who complete academic programs, many enter the field of environmental health through training in the Army and Navy as preventive medicine technicians.

For those who find they need environmental health training in mid-career, the National Environmental Health Association has begun offering a one-week course in the management of hazardous substances. The course, which is given at locations around the country, leads to an RHSP certification, Registered Hazardous Substance Professional.

Resources

The National Hospice Organization provides an employment referral service for members. For information, write 1901 North Moore Street, Arlington, Virginia 22209. Phone (703) 243-5900. For additional reading, see *On Death and Dying* by Elizabeth

Kubler-Ross (Macmillan, $5.95) and *The Hospice Movement* by Sandol Stoddard (Random House, $4.95).

For further information on other specialties, consult individual health care professional societies. **The American Dental Association** is at 211 East Chicago Avenue, Chicago, Illinois 60611. **The American Medical Association** is at 515 North State Street, Chicago, Illinois 60610. **The American Nurses' Association** is at 2420 Pershing Road, Kansas City, Missouri 64108. **The American College of Healthcare Executives** is at 840 North Lake Shore Drive, Chicago, Illinois 60611.

For information on careers in health care administration, contact Dennis Barnhardt at the **Medical Group Management Association,** 104 Inverness Terrace East, Englewood, Colorado 80112-5306. Phone: (303) 799-1111.

To learn more about **Eric Dunlop's** courses in biotechnology, contact him at the **Colorado Bioprocessing Center,** Colorado State University, Fort Collins, Colorado 80523. Phone: (303) 491-4590. Look for other graduate courses of this kind in the engineering, microbiology, or business departments of major universities.

The Association of Biotechnology Companies is at 1120 Vermont Avenue, N.W., Suite 601, Washington, D.C. 20005. Phone: (202) 842-2229.

There are three principal organizations in the environmental health field. **The American Industrial Hygiene Association** is at P.O. Box 8390, 345 White Pond Drive, Akron, Ohio 44320. Phone: (216) 873-2442. **The National Environmental Health Association** is located at 720 South Colorado Boulevard, Suite 970: South Tower, Denver, Colorado 80222. Phone: (303) 756-9090. **The Society of Toxicology** is at 1133 15th Street, N.W., Suite 1000, Washington, D.C. 20005. Phone: (202) 371-1393.

Chapter Twelve

Information Professions

The new information economy is beginning to create some innovative job roles. As in other fields, it's easier to spot the new skills in information management than it is the new job titles. The occupations are still evolving.

One rising job, the data base manager, seems to be growing out of secretarial functions. Another, the information broker, is a spin-off from library careers; law librarians are a mixture of two fields. Meanwhile, the chief information officer, a corporate job role, seems less certain to take hold—like corporate managerial jobs in general.

✦ ✦ ✦

Information Brokers

I was sitting in the Portland airport, browsing through the business section of the *Oregonian*, when Annette Mathias' advertisement caught my eye.

"ASK US ANYTHING," the ad dared.

It went on to explain that Mathias, an information broker, could research virtually any field under the sun. Intrigued, I called her up.

Mathias described what she does and gave me a thumbnail sketch of her career. She'd been trained as a medical librarian in Cleveland and had worked for years in a local hospital. Then she founded a small freelance research business in her home. One client led to another, and the business grew. Today, Information Specialists has four divisions in six offices and grosses three million dollars a year. Now Mathias lives and works in Portland, communicating by phone and fax with the headquarters of the company she founded back in Cleveland. She sold the firm but retained the portion she runs.

Mathias is one of an estimated one thousand independent librarians who are revolutionizing the ways Americans procure information. They're a profession with loose ties to the traditional world of librarians. Like most other information professionals, their job titles are still evolving. Some are known as "infopreneurs," or special librarians. It's a field that has grown up with computers.

Information brokers earn their living by navigating computer-supported data bases, which are multiplying rapidly. There now are somewhere between five thousand and ten thousand bases worldwide. The profession is growing just as fast. Membership in the Special Libraries Association has tripled in the past seven years and is expected to double again by the end of the decade. A smaller group of special librarians who are in business for themselves, the Association of Independent Information Professionals, has been growing at 30 percent a year. Those are the "infopreneurs."

Data bases are stores of information founded by specialists in a given field—say, civil engineering. In that sense, they're nothing new. But computer technology has multiplied the amount of data that can be stored, while providing tools for plowing through it many times more efficiently than before. Obviously, in a world of five to ten thousand data bases, constantly proliferating, it's easy to get lost. To search the data successfully, one needs to know where to look efficiently. That's where the vendors come in. Vendors are data base brokers.

The principal data bases are wholesaled by third-party vendors such as Dialog, a Knight-Ridder company based in Palo Alto, California. Dialog carries about four hundred of the major data bases, which subscribers can access for a fee. Here the issue of cost becomes crucial.

Data base searches typically cost $1.00 to $1.50 per minute, in addition to telephone charges and the cost of reproducing articles. Even within a defined set of data bases, such as Dialog, expenses can mount up quickly. One of the major factors in cost containment is the caliber of modem a researcher uses. Experts say that a high-speed modem can pay for itself in a matter of weeks.

It's the need for efficiency that has spurred the growth of special librarians. Mathias' firm charges a flat rate for research (typically $50 an hour) and sets a "not-to-exceed" ceiling price before a project begins. Information Specialists boasts access to 1,500 data bases through its various vendors. Other firms' fees vary, depending upon the nature of the research and the resources required.

As one might expect, the range of products that special librarians investigate is phenomenal. One famous story in the trade concerns a scientist in a chemical company who came up with the notion of marketing synthetic eggs. He'd worked out all the technology and found it was possible to produce everything from yolk to egg shell artificially.

The question was whether the project was practical. Was it economical to create eggs in the laboratory? The company hired an information broker to conduct a search of data bases in the field of food technology. Eureka! The info broker found that, in fact, someone had already filed for a patent on artificial eggs. But the process had never been commercialized. The next step was to determine why. The researcher checked out prices for the chemicals required and found that artificial eggs would cost several times the chicken-laid variety. After a few hours' research, the company had the information it needed to put the project on hold. (Reported by Suzanne Mattingly and Robin Clark in the Dialog publication, *Inside Business*. July, 1989.)

Mathias' firm has investigated everything from firms engaged in refurbishing hotels (for a manufacturer of bathtub enclosures) to the employee insurance policies of Fortune 500 companies. In the latter case, a client was interested in knowing how many companies covered payments for the treatment of alcoholism.

Special librarians have begun to coin their own lingo, in the process of sifting through their data. Here are several key terms.

+ *Data* are simple facts and figures—the raw stuff with which data base researchers work.

+ *Information* is intelligible data: for example, economic figures cast in the form of Gross National Product.

+ *Knowledge* or *Intelligence* is useful information applicable to the problem at hand. The final product of a search, which summarizes such information, is referred to as an "intelligence report."

Typically, there are three major parties to any data base search transaction:

+ The *Vendor*, or wholesaler of the data base,

+ The *Searcher* (the special librarian, infopreneur, or information broker), and

+ The *End User* of the intelligence, who pays the fee.

Other trade-talk phrases include:

+ *Mapping*: the process of winnowing through data,
+ *Nesting*: locating one concept within another, as one narrows the search, and
+ *False Drop*: coming up with bad information.

One large question confronting special librarians concerns how much expertise their work actually requires. Vendors are beginning to devise user-friendly formats that can be learned in a day. Dialog offers one-day seminars to new customers at no charge.

The market for end-user training will probably grow, as more Americans become comfortable with on-line information services such as CompuServe and Prodigy. Consumers who have learned to scan airline fares and schedules on one of those home computer programs have a good start on learning to search more complicated data bases. In addition, some analysts point out that much of the data carried by vendors such as Dialog is widely available for free. Public libraries have much of it in print form and on compact disks.

Thus, with a bit of training, non-librarians could learn to ferret out quite a lot of information for themselves. That's why the wave of the future may be to provide certain staff members of an organization with basic training in data base searching, so that they can meld those skills with specialized knowledge of their industry. Again, the trend seems to be to add skills to an existing job rather than creating a new occupation that pervades many other fields. Observers note that the relatively new profession of chief information officer (CIO) has failed to take hold in the corporate world. They speculate that special librarians could suffer the same fate, if user-friendly vendors such as Dialog have their way. Meanwhile, however, the ranks of full-time information brokers are steadily growing.

Law Librarians

One of the fastest-growing infotrades is in law libraries, which are revolutionizing legal practices. As Americans file lawsuits in record numbers, legal information and legal librarians have multiplied accordingly, with the numbers of law librarians tripling in the past fifteen years. At last count there were five thousand people working in this field across the country. Most of the growth is in law firms, law schools, and corporate legal departments.

The field is still so new that few graduate library schools as yet offer a degree in law librarianship. (The University of Washington and the University of California at Berkeley have well-recognized programs.) However, half the nation's library schools now offer at least one course in the subject. Most jobs require a master of library science degree. Head librarians may have both an MLS and a degree in law.

Mark Estes, a law librarian at a large law firm and president of the American Association of Law Librarians, fell into his field by accident—literally. He was a law school student, attending classes part time while training for the 1976 Olympic Games as a bicycle racer. Shortly before the Olympic tryouts, Estes crashed. His injuries were serious enough that there was no time to recover and get back in condition for training.

Estes found himself with an extra term in law school. He enjoyed research and decided to look into library science. Today he supervises a large staff in a rapidly changing field, one that has been transformed repeatedly by computers.

"Two months after I got here, we subscribed to an on-line data base," he recalls. "I was still learning that process when six months later we got our own system. Now the new technology is CD-ROMs: bookshelves of material on a single compact disk, electronically scanned."

The new information technology is more and more user-friendly. LEXIS, one of the most popular data bases in law, now offers a "mouse" pointer to minimize typing. Could computerized research eliminate the need for specially trained law librarians?

Estes sees no signs that his field is slacking. "Data base searching isn't as easy as it seems," he says. "You have to know what you're looking for. Even if lawyers can learn to use more of this technology themselves, I believe librarians will take over more teaching functions. They'll help attorneys target their research and refine their questions. As the volume of legal information grows, the trick will be not to get lost in it."

Analysts at the U.S. Department of Labor believe that other professional roles may be in the offing. The use of computers in mapping, for instance, could give rise to geographic information specialists who will create, store, and retrieve data for forecasting weather, planning emergency operations, and managing land use. As with most fields, the key is to concentrate on specific skills rather than full-blown occupations. Look for courses in data base searching within progressive library science schools or departments of technical communication.

Data Base Managers

The same process can be seen in one other data-related job function that seems to be growing in importance: data base management. Data base administrators help design their organizations' computer systems and maintain the systems day by day. They oversee data entry and maintain security and access to the files. When a computer system needs upgrading, it's usually the data-base adminstrator who takes the lead in making plans for a new one.

Data base administration is a good, ground-level, hands-on occupation. While not every organization can afford a chief information officer, every company needs someone to maintain the mailing list, update payroll files, and generally look out for its data.

This is an interesting field when it comes to training. Many of the basic skills in data base administration can be learned by mastering common software programs such as LotusWorks or dBASE III Plus. Data base management is the kind of skill that lends itself to job-related training, although as anyone who has worked with dBASE or Lotus programs will attest, those aren't the kinds of skills that can be learned over a lunch hour. Most people need some additional classes, which are widely available.

Some secretaries and other clerical workers have found it possible to upgrade their jobs by learning additional skills in data base management. Those who are able to carve out a full-time niche may find good learning opportunities, as the scope of the field seems to be expanding. According to Dr. Gary Marchionini of the University of Maryland, "Many administrators find themselves working with other media, such as video and electronic mail, in addition to computers. Plus, there's a whole new market for value-added services. Lots of organizations now sell their data bases—not just the information in them but the design of their data base as well. Ameritech, the regional phone company, recently bought two library cataloging systems to manage some of the new information products they expect to market."

Marchionini teaches a course on media services management that is broadcast nationwide by Jones International, a cable television company. Jones' Mind Extension University offers a full master's degree program in educational technology leadership from George Washington University. For information, call 1-800-777-MIND.

Information Networking
A related field with a somewhat more high-tech emphasis is information networking, an occupation based on the increasing use of computers to transmit as well as compile information. Jay Gillette, a

senior fellow at the Center for the New West, illustrates the field this way.

"Think of a car dealership where the product is constantly changing. The parts department has to keep a data base inventory for every old model. The sales staff needs to know about upcoming model changes. Plus, they need to keep track of who their customers are and what kinds of features they want in their cars. That way, they can give input to the engineers who are designing next year's model.

"Someone has to keep track of all that circulating data and organize it into useful information. In the future, more companies will employ information managers or local area network (LAN) managers to design and connect computer operations."

According to scientists at Carnegie Mellon University, the information will soon involve pictures as well as words and numbers. Consider this scenario, which should appear within the next few years. A critically ill patient is brought to the emergency room of a hospital. The patient carries a computerized "smart card" containing his medical history. Scanning the card, the attending physician notes that a CAT scan and X-rays were taken a month earlier. Using the card to order visual images, he calls up the patient's hometown physician and the doctors confer by phone while watching the CAT scan and X-ray images (all within minutes). Following treatment, the patient's insurance carrier is billed via the smart card.

The skills for information networking come from several fields: computer science, telecommunications, and business management. Basically, they involve knowing how to design and manage information systems and how to link telephone and computer technology. (Of course, says Gillette, it also helps to know how to read critically and write clearly; information technology is simply a high-tech version of the Three-Rs.)

In 1989, Carnegie Mellon launched the first Information Networking Institute in the country. It's a fourteen-month master's degree program for people with a bachelor's degree in electrical engineering, computer science, or a related discipline.

For those who can't get away to Pittsburgh, Gillette recommends a couple of other paths to build information networking skills. One can learn to access data bases by computer modem through a commercial information service such as Prodigy or CompuServe.

Resources

For additional information on employment and training, contact these professional associations.

The Special Libraries Association, 1700 18th Street, NW, Washington, D.C. 20009. Phone (202) 234-4700.

The Association of Independent Information Professionals, 801 Arch Street, Philadelphia, Pennsylvania 19107. Phone: (215) 823-5490.

The Information Industry Association sponsors numerous conferences and publications. They are at 555 New Jersey Avenue, N.W., Suite 800, Washington, D.C. 20001. Phone: (202) 639-8262.

The phone number for **Dialog** is 1-800-334-2564. Two other prominent vendors are **Mead Data Central** (publishers of legal data bases LEXIS and NEXIS) at 1-800-325-8227 and **Dow Jones** at (609) 452-1511.

For information on careers in law librarianship, contact the **American Association of Law Libraries** at 53 West Jackson Boulevard, Suite 940, Chicago, Illinois 60604. Phone: (312) 939-4764.

Courses in local area networking are available from telecommunications training facilities such as **Bellcore Tech,** (800) TEACH-ME, and vendors such as **Vovell,** (800) 526-5463. Information on the **Carnegie Mellon** program is available at (412) 268-5721.

Chapter Thirteen

International Trade

Employment in international trade is growing rapidly as the global economy takes hold. Between 1985 and 1991 the volume of U.S. exports almost doubled, from $230 billion to $450 per year. But economic statistics don't tell the whole story of this dynamic field. Many people who are pursuing a career in international business have deep commitments to the prospect of building a better world through global trade. In this chapter we'll meet some of these individuals and consider both the practical and the visionary sides of their field.

◆　◆　◆

Doing Business Overseas

There are some extraordinary figures in the global marketplace. One of them is Dikembe Mutombo, the seven-foot-two, second-year center for the Denver Nuggets of the National Basketball Association. He's from the west-African nation of Zaire.

Not that foreign-born basketball players are unusual in the United States. Mutombo has plenty of company. Currently there are 22 players in the NBA who were born outside the United States, plus another 135 players from other countries on the rosters of major American colleges and universities.

But Mutombo is no ordinary athlete. A graduate of Georgetown University with a degree in linguistics and diplomacy, Mutombo speaks seven languages and has recorded a TV commercial for McDonalds in which he touts a giant-sized burger (the "Mutombo Jumbo") in five of them. He's also learning to use his image overseas. Last summer he spent several weeks in Europe marketing his personal line of sports clothes, "Mutombo 55"—his number with the Nuggets. Then he accepted an invitation from

CARE, the international relief organization, to visit camps for Somalian refugees in Kenya. Mutombo is an active spokesman for CARE and has joined their board of directors.

"If God can give me the chance, I want to play basketball for maybe another ten years," he says. "But basketball is not what I want to do for the rest of my life. Maybe someday I'll be working for the World Bank, the U.N., or CARE. Right now I'm just preparing myself."

While Mutombo is an individual of unusual proportions—not everyone is seven-two and speaks seven languages—he's typical of many people who are discovering that the market for their skills is worldwide. What's needed is the ability to make connection overseas. That's where international trade consultants such as Windham Loopesko come in. Loopesko is part of a growing network of international trade specialists who link companies with global products and services to worldwide markets. It's a relatively new field, where skills and jobs are still evolving. Some of the most vital skills involve the complicated logistics of doing business in countries with different currencies and cultures.

According to Loopesko, international trade involves procedures that are common to other businesses. To be successful, you must: (1) understand your customers' needs; (2) know how to deliver your product (including knowing the regulatory and other obstacles you may encounter); and (3) know how to sell your product and train dealers in customer service. The main difference is that overseas trade is more complex. "That's why the commitment to doing business overseas must be long term," he says. "It always takes more time, energy, and money than you think."

Skills are changing as the field grows. Some professionals, like Loopesko, are specialists in the logistics of international business and/or the economy of a particular region. Loopesko concentrates on trade with Europe. His clients include a French firm with a weight reduction product that purportedly takes off five pounds in a few days, and an Italian company with a device to cleanse factory smoke while converting it to energy. They represent the kinds of value that can be generated by international trade.

In addition to independent consultants, some international trade specialists are employed by large corporations that do business abroad. For corporate employees, the trend seems to favor acquiring a few basic skills in international trade and grafting them onto another business specialty. For example, someone with a degree in marketing or finance might take a few courses in export marketing covering methods of payment, financing, licensing, shipping, and insurance. A recent survey of employers by the American Graduate School of International Management in Arizona, commonly known as the Thunderbird School, found that most companies were inclined to hire people with that kind of background rather than international trade professionals who might spend their entire careers overseas.

Graduate Education in the Field

The Thunderbird School is a pioneer in the field of international business education. Founded after World War II on a civilian air base that had been appropriated by the military, the school first enrolled combat pilots who wanted to prepare for new careers. The first president was a general who had directed a flight school on the air base. He bought the airfield and its buildings for one dollar, then raised $175,000 to launch the international business program.

Today the Thunderbird School is still somewhat underfunded, and isolated in a northwest suburb of Phoenix. But in the quality of its training and its commitment to international education, Thunderbird is probably unmatched. The school enrolls about a thousand students at a time, a third of them from foreign countries. Many others are veterans of the Peace Corps. Life on campus is abuzz with ethnic festivals, seminars on foreign affairs, and conversations in every language under the sun.

Students spend a year taking courses in three areas: modern languages (nine are offered), international studies, and world business. Most earn an MIM degree; that's a Master's of International Management. The degree has been proliferating all across the country in recent years, but it's identified most closely with Thunderbird.

In addition, with twenty-three thousand alumni all over the world, Thunderbird offers a natural network for practitioners of international trade.

Short-term Training

For those who want to master a specific subject, such as shipping, while holding on to their jobs, the World Trade Center network offers excellent resources. The original World Trade Center, based in New York City, founded the network of related organizations in 1968, essentially as franchises of the WTC. Today there are 272 World Trade Center affiliates all around the world, from Abidjan to Zurich. The centers are locally run and they vary in services and facilities, but many offer up-to-date information on business opportunities and an ongoing round of short courses.

A typical one-day workshop might go something like this. Subject: export methods of payment. Leader: the vice president of the international division of a large local bank. Topics: What is a letter of credit? How does it work? What are the risks? When should it be used? How is one composed?

Recently the World Trade Institute, an affiliate of the World Trade Center, has created a Certificate in International Trade. The certificate is intended to show that the bearer has completed and been tested in a standard curriculum relating to all facets of international trade. To give an idea of the range of skills emerging in this field, here are the required courses for the certificate program.

In Importing: Customs Brokerage, Importing Techniques, Export-Import Letters of Credit, Fundamentals of Building an Import Business, Customs Entry Preparation, Import Transportation.

In Exporting: Export Documentation, Export-Import Letters of Credit, Introduction to Export Marketing and Promotion, Essentials of Establishing an Export Business, Case Problems in Export Management. All of that is in addition to a required course, Introduction to World Trade.

The program is another example of trade and professional associations assuming education and credentialing functions that once were the sole province of colleges and universities. As the course titles indicate, they're performing that function in part because of the specificity of hands-on skills and knowledge that emerging professions such as international trade require.

Finding a Job Overseas

In addition to trading in goods and services, there's one other important commodity to consider exporting, and that's oneself. Whether prompted by a desire to serve or to escape the recession, many Americans have been considering avenues to employment overseas.

Recently I sat in on a seminar by an international sales and marketing consultant, John Slater, on "How to Get a Job Overseas." It's a subject that Slater knows well. In 1980, he retired from a twenty-year career in the U.S. Marine Corps with a freshly minted MBA in real estate management earned while he was stationed in San Diego. When he mustered out of the Marines and tried to find employment in San Diego in the midst of a recession, he discovered there were no real estate jobs in sight.

Slater began networking in other fields, talking about civilian employment with anyone he could find. He came across a fellow veteran who referred him to a recruiting firm specializing in recycling military veterans overseas. That's how Slater found his way to Saudi Arabia. For the next several years he spent most of his time traipsing across the desert, instructing Bedouin tribesmen in the fine points of guarding oil derricks.

It was not the kind of work he'd planned to do with his MBA. But Slater spent his vacations networking in Turkey, cultivating international business contacts. Finally he landed a job there and developed a sales and marketing seminar for bank personnel.

Today Slater is well established as an international consultant. He has conducted training seminars in Turkey, Saudi Arabia, Poland, and Greece. His most recent assignment was in Lagos, Nigeria. It was the result of a contact he'd made three jobs ago with a banker from England.

Slater stresses the importance of networking when looking for work overseas. He believes that it's important to spend vacation times scouting new assignments, and not to burn any bridges, even if one is fired from an overseas job unexpectedly.

"Don't expect a stable career overseas," he cautions. "Contracts can be broken at any time. If you're employed teaching technical skills to native workers, consider how quickly they'll catch on. That's how soon you'll be out of a job."

But one assignment can lead to another. Furthermore, working overseas does not preclude pursuing a career in the United States. For consultants such as Slater, the two markets go hand in hand. Overseas networking is simply a way to expand one's market.

Slater says it's best to research international jobs while in the United States. Otherwise you may end up playing Catch 22 in a foreign country: To get a job, you first must have a work permit; but to get a work permit, you first must have a job.

The basic skills are networking and doing your homework.

Resources

The Thunderbird International Graduate School of Management is at 15249 North 59th Avenue, Glendale, Arizona 85306-6005. Phone: (602) 978-7210.

For information on **World Trade Center** offices that sponsor educational programs, and the new certificate program in international trade, contact **The World Trade Institute**, One World Trade Center, 55th Floor West, New York, New York 10048. Phone: (212) 435-2562.

John Slater recommends the following books on overseas employment: *The Complete Guide to International Jobs and Careers*

($13.95) and *The Almanac of International Jobs and Careers* ($14.95). Both are by Ronald and Caryl Krannich and published by Impact Publications of Virginia.

Teaching English Abroad by Susan Griffith ($13.95) is another useful book. The publisher is Peterson's Guides. So is *Work, Study, Travel Abroad* by the Council on International Educational Exchange ($12.95), published by St. Martin's Press.

The International Employment Gazette is a recommended periodical, available at $3.95 per issue. Phone (800) 882-9188.

For information on John Slater's seminars, call (303) 850-0246.

Chapter Fourteen

Residential Management

Changing patterns in the U.S. economy and new lifestyles are creating new opportunities in the American labor market. Housing is one growth field, as professional specialists take on some of the responsibilities families once carried.

In this chapter, three emerging job roles are profiled: the access coordinator for the elderly, the apartment manager, and the household manager. All three fields are growing in professionalism, with more emphasis on formal training and with salary figures that contain some surprises.

❖ ❖ ❖

For those who believe in planning their careers by watching trends, there's one development in the United States that's hard to ignore. It's the incredible rate at which households have been multiplying. According to *Philadelphia Inquirer* reporters Donald Barlett and James Steele, the number of individuals filing income-tax returns as heads of households has grown from one million to twelve million since 1960.

In their book, *America: What Went Wrong?*, the reporters note that whereas in 1960 almost two-thirds of tax returns were submitted by married couples, by 1989 the percentage was less than half. It's a trend that's fueled by several factors: rising numbers of single parents, adults postponing marriage, and elderly citizens living longer. Households seem to be a booming cottage industry.

But what do they have to do with employment? Quite a lot, if we look at the question of where and how Americans are living in these independent households, especially as they grow older. Consider the statistics. In 1980, the number of people in the U.S. aged sixty-five and older was about twenty-eight million. By the year 2000, that figure will increase another 20 percent to thirty-five million. Meanwhile, people continue to live longer. In a recent thirteen-year period, life expectancy increased by four years for both males and females. And the end is not in sight; longevity is still increasing. So, proportionally, are the numbers of "extreme elderly"—persons age 85 and up. That group tripled in a recent twenty-five-year period.

Independence for the Elderly

For federal housing authorities, these are potent figures. Currently, three million elderly Americans live in apartment complexes that were built with federal subsidies. The housing provides subsidized rent for those over age sixty, if they meet certain income guidelines and remain "independent." Independence is the crucial factor, and not just because of rent subsidies. It's also a matter of lifestyle. Elderly people who can live on their own do not require the costly, confining services of nursing homes. The key to cost containment and quality of life for older Americans is the ability to manage on their own.

That's why there's an occupation taking shape that is likely to grow, by one title or another, in the years ahead. It's the job we read about in chapter 4: the specialist in independent elder-life. Remember the case of Laurel Olson?

Oli Wigington is a good example of this new professional worker. A fifty-five-year-old ex-school teacher, Wigington serves as an Access Coordinator for the Elderly, or ACE, for the Colorado Housing and Finance Authority. She learned about the ACE program after landing a job as manager of an apartment building.

CHFA had established the program to meet two needs. It wanted to provide support services for extremely elderly residents while also generating employment for young-elderly human service workers such as Wigington. Herb Angle, who started the ACE program, said, "We wanted maturity in this role. That's why we sought early retirees from service professions such as teaching.

"In addition, we also knew that there were plenty of people in their fifties and sixties who were finding jobs hard to come by. It seemed a natural match: keeping the elderly independent and keeping some good human service workers employed."

Wigington's job is to watch over a client pool of 370 elderly residents in three apartment complexes. She serves as a broker for special services such as transportation, housecleaning, medical referrals, and companionship. With an active case load of twenty-five to thirty clients at any time, she helps residents find particular resources as needs arise.

Wigington says that her age is a decided asset in this process: "If I were some young dynamo just out of school, I wouldn't have any credibility with these older people. And the experience I've had working in a service profession is helpful, too. I use a lifetime of skills every day."

The ACE program has been specially funded in ten states by the Robert Wood Johnson Foundation. It's a pilot project, intended to demonstrate the cost effectiveness of helping senior citizens remain independent. Eventually apartment complex owners are expected to take over funding.

In other states the title of Wigington's job may be different. It's one of the 33 percent of today's jobs that are still evolving. But given the combined trends of independent households and aging citizens, positions such as Access Coordinator for the Elderly look to be a major trend of social service jobs in the future.

Managing Apartments

Apartment management is a similar field. I learned about it from Marsha McVey, a long-time instructor in secretarial studies at a community college outside Denver. McVey and her husband had followed an interesting route to residential management. Back in the late 1970s, they'd decided to invest in several apartment buildings. That was just before the energy industry collapsed and the local economy went in a tailspin. Their timing could not have been worse.

As unemployed oil industry workers exited Denver and vacancy rates soared, apartment foreclosures tripled in a single year. The McVeys found themselves scrambling to hang onto tenants. Then their prospects turned worse. Larry McVey lost his job as an oil and gas accountant.

That's when Marsha had an insight. For some time, she'd been watching droves of new students enroll at her community college. Many were single mothers seeking new careers as secretaries. But given the condition of Denver's economy, it was not clear where they'd find work when they completed their secretarial studies.

At the same time she was concerned about her students, Marsha was wrestling with her own problems. With competition so keen for tenants, she and Larry needed more highly skilled apartment managers. It wasn't enough to employ people who knew how to collect rent and call plumbers. They needed managers with strong skills in customer service, and sales ability to sign up new tenants.

One day the light dawned. Suppose she were to start a special curriculum in apartment management . . . .

She did. Today the Residential Property Management program at Arapahoe Community College has trained several hundred students in a curriculum that includes a broad array of subjects: building maintenance, tenant law, computer-supported accounting, dispute resolution, and customer service.

In building maintenance, the primary objective is not to train students in performing major repairs but to help them become sophisticated consumers of craft trades. Students learn basic principles of heating and air conditioning, plumbing, and electrical and security systems. That way they can learn whom to call and when, and use outside services more effectively.

Residential management salaries vary by region and according to the kind of facility run. A new manager in a hundred-unit building may earn $12,000 a year plus free housing, while an experienced manager handling six hundred units may make $26,000. Property managers who oversee a half-dozen residential managers can earn $50,000 and up.

I interviewed one of Marsha McVey's graduates and found that she had doubled her salary in two years while completing the community college program. When she began her courses, she was a leasing representative at five dollars an hour. When she finished, she was in a salaried position in management, making $22,000 a year.

The program has been good for the McVeys as well. "It's been a chance to teach what we learned while losing half our apartments in the 80's," says Marsha. "Even if we don't have any money left, we gained a lot of knowledge!"

"But we could have lost our money in oil wells with a lot less brain damage," adds Larry.

Household Management

A third kind of residential management is emerging from another trend—the change in economic lifestyles of married couples. In 1940, husbands were the sole wage earners in 60 percent of American families. But by 1981, three-quarters of the families had working wives as well. Most couples need more than one job to maintain a middle-class lifestyle in today's economy. This new dual-career lifestyle has created new employment of a sort, as other occupations have evolved to meet the needs of working couples. For parents there was child care: a fast-growing service that soon became franchised. Supermarket delicatessens flourished, with their microwave meals. So did housecleaning services, another industry that lent itself to franchising.

All these industries offer low-wage employment typical of America's fast-growing service sector. But others—such as the access coordinators for the elderly and apartment managers—actually provide a decent livelihood. And in the case of household management, our third field, pay scales border on the impressive.

Household management is not a new idea; the field has been around as long as maids and butlers. But in 1980s America it began to grow. In part that's because America's upper-income families did so well. According to the authors of *America: What Went Wrong?* salaries of people earning more than one million dollars increased a whopping 2,184 percent during the eighties.

Those who lagged behind a bit in income, earning between $200,000 and a million dollars annually, increased 697 percent. With incomes of that magnitude, plenty of Americans entered the high-end housing market.

The other factor in the growth of household management had to do with a subtle change in social values. There seemed to be a revival of interest in the social graces. Sandy Wischmeyer, who directed an education program in household management, traces the change back to the 1960s.

"I think we're just recovering from the counterculture," she says. "It seems we went through a period of twenty years when we lost contact with tradition. But people want structure today; they want to know what's right. That's why you're seeing more books published on etiquette." Wischmeyer understands that transition. A former junior-high-school physical-education teacher, she ran a river-rafting program for several years before discovering the field of household management.

It's an industry that seems to appeal to career-changers. Mary Starkey, who established an academy for household management several years ago, came to the field through a series of jobs in social services. Frustrated at what she saw as a lack of results in the public-service sector, she eventually quit to found her own employment agency. The first person who called her was someone looking for a job as a nanny. She found that person a job, then received calls from others who were interested in similar positions. She founded a housekeeping service in addition to her job placement agency.

Salaries weren't bad. Entry-level household managers make an average of $18,000 a year, plus living expenses. As she investigated the field, she found a number of educators in it. One former high-school physics teacher was making $65,000 a year managing a mansion in the south Denver suburbs. Another, in Denver's posh Polo Club area, was a former college home economics professor with a PhD. Starkey found that, for experienced and capable people, $30,000 to $40,000 salaries were common.

Unlike more tradition-oriented societies such as England, American household managers seem to change assignments frequently. Eighteen months to two years in a given home is typical. That's one reason it's a good field for retired couples, career changers, and others in mid-life transition. Starkey points out that displaced homemakers, for instance, can find a new niche in household management. "We've been through several decades of downgrading the domestic image," she says. "Now, nobody wants to be a homemaker. But somebody has to take care of making a home.

"So we're back to a new division of labor. That's what the profession of household management means to displaced homemakers. We're giving a section of life back to somebody who knows how to handle it."

The Starkey International Institute curriculum is a smorgasbord of skills in everything from silverware polishing to diplomatic protocol. It's an eight-week program, 8 a.m. to 5 p.m. every day. Classes are held in a nineteenth-century mansion that looks as if it was designed for a Victorian murder mystery, a Charles Addams cartoon, or, at the very least, high tea.

Starkey's catalog includes courses in housecleaning; entertaining (including flower arranging, decorating, and formal tea service); home repairs; inside and outside maintenance; staff supervision; and the care of fine china, crystal, silverware, pewter, and fine art. Students learn how to care for linoleum floors, how a piece of silver looks when it needs to be redipped, how to address public officials, and how to make bite-sized hors d'oeuvres.

How stable is the field of household management? Like the nanny industry, the household business is a product of America's rising nouveau riche. If income becomes more equally distributed in a society that lacks a traditional servant class, will the occupations of nanny and butler survive?

It's hard to say. But meanwhile there's an obvious new niche in the market for displaced homemakers and other domestic engineers. "We're giving value to what women have done all their lives," says Starkey. "For the right person, it's a field with tremendous opportunities. The important thing is that people enjoy bringing tasks to completion, and that they love providing a service."

Resources

For more information on the household management program, write to the **Starkey International Institute**, 1410 High Street, Denver, Colorado 80218. Phone: (303) 394-4904.

To learn more about the **Residential Property Management Program at Arapahoe Community College**, call (303) 794-1550.

The **Colorado Housing and Finance Authority**, sponsors of the **Access Coordinators for the Elderly** program, is at (303) 297-2432.

Chapter Fifteen

Teaching and Updating Technical Skills

For most Americans, today's pace of constant technological change is a mixed blessing. While we may enjoy the convenience of new appliances and marvel at the prospect of new inventions, most of us are still a bit overwhelmed by it all.

In this chapter we'll consider some new skills and occupations that are intended to help more people make better use of new technology. We'll also track new developments in the education of technical professionals, focusing on engineers.

◆ ◆ ◆

Ken Davis makes a living helping people operate their VCRs. For anyone who has tried to decipher the manual that came with a video cassette recorder, his job makes sense. Davis recently retired from the U.S. Air Force, where he worked in electronics, and saw a business opportunity in the civilian world. In a sense, the challenge was no different from his work in the military. Davis explains, "The Air Force uses highly technical terms in teaching, and you're supposed to understand that. But people don't."

A lot of VCR owners could sympathize. According to T. Heymann, author of the 1991 *Unofficial U.S. Census*, only 36 million of the estimated 179 million Americans who own video cassette recorders know how to program them. As a result, says Davis, most owners of a $600 VCR can probably operate only $200 worth of the equipment. Davis says, "I learned to break things down into simple steps. If you break it down into simple steps, people understand. They're not idiots."

Instructional Technology
The formal name for the field in which Davis has found himself is

instructional technology. It's a growing field, filled with all sorts of new skills and terminology: authoring, knowledge navigation, multi-media data bases, hypertext, voice output computers, and TDDs. That's "telephone devices for the deaf."

Instructional technology is one of the fastest-rising fields around: not just for full-time educators, but for people in other professions who need to learn how to train others effectively. To suggest how the field is growing, one of the leading professional groups—the National Society for Performance and Instruction—has attracted five thousand members in the thirty years it's been in existence.

It's hard to escape technological change. The other day I found a laminated card on the sidewalk. It must have fallen from a salesman's pocket. It was the mission statement of Sunbeam-Oster, a manufacturing company. The card listed the firm's "five keys to success." I read the card as I walked along, and item one caught my eye: "Over the past several years, approximately 21 percent of Sunbeam-Oster's sales were from new products developed in the past four years . . . . The company's objective is to reach close to 30 percent . . . ."

I considered what that statement means, not only to the people who work at Sunbeam-Oster, constantly devising new products, but also to the consumers who'll have to learn to operate all those new devices. One of the difficulties in connecting with new machines is that most of them require strong reading skills; yet literacy levels in this country are dropping. Household newspaper subscriptions, for example, have fallen 20 percent in the past twenty years. So one of the prime challenges to instructional technology specialists has been to come up with alternatives to print-based instructions.

That's one of the ways in which the field has shifted radically from the old days of audio-visual learning aids, such as filmstrips. The revolution occurred in the mid-1980s, when manufacturers introduced a new generation of microcomputers such as the Apple Macintosh. These powerful micros combined illustrated menus and graphics with immense stores of memory. Then video laser disks added another visual dimension, with even larger memory lodes.

In the 1990s, text was combined with graphics and full-motion video to create another new generation of multimedia programs. IBM introduced the first set of programs in 1991: a series of literature studies on Alfred Lord Tennyson's poem, "Ulysses," Shakespeare's *Hamlet*, Martin Luther King Jr.'s "Letter from the Birmingham City Jail," and *Black Elk Speaks*.

The programs are stunning. Students can click a mouse at any point in the "Ulysses" program, for example, and tap into a one-hundred-hour multimedia data base on the poem. The data base includes a detailed history of the Trojan War, on which the poems of Tennyson and Homer were based, and an assortment of actors reading lines with different interpretations.

That's the real benefit of multimedia. It's not just static text. Multimedia can compete for the attention of jaded teenagers raised on MTV. In addition, the programs are interactive. By involving students in actively researching data bases—a process known as "knowledge navigation"—multimedia technology multiplies the effectiveness of learning. Studies have shown that students retain about 10 percent of what they see; 50 percent of what they see and hear; and 80 percent of what they see, hear, and do.

Multimedia could revolutionize primary and secondary education. It's an alternative to processing students through passive, traditional high-school classes. Long-range, however, the greatest impact of multimedia may occur not in the schools but in the workplace. That's good news for employers who are caught between declining levels of literacy and jobs that require higher skills. Studies by the U.S. Department of Defense indicate that multimedia learning is 40 percent more effective than traditional training, with a 30-percent greater retention rate and a learning curve that's 30 percent shorter.

Texas State Technical College at Waco, a high-tech training institute, has a fascinating experiment underway: teaching basic skills to support staff workers. The college has created a special curriculum in basic math, the physical sciences, and English communication for its groundskeepers, housekeepers, and custodians—many of whom were high-school dropouts. The program uses video laser disks with dramatized lessons on fractions, decimals, and percentages. A typical lesson might focus on using math to mix industrial solvents at the proper strength, finding the correct formula through different methods of calculation. The actors in the videos are the workers themselves.

Students can develop their basic skills through an array of learning options. There are computer keyboard-based programs, cassette tapes, and televised programs, as well as texts. The idea is to offer several options so that individuals can work in their own best learning styles. By studying individually, they also can reduce their fears of failure, based on earlier experiences in school. For those who don't type, touch screens are available to guide students through the lessons.

"We don't want any student to have an excuse not to learn,"

says Don Goodwin, the president of the college.

The learning materials are produced in a million-dollar laboratory on campus, where faculty can learn to create customized computer and laser disk programs for their classes. It's a technique known as "authoring."

Today there are thirty to forty different commercial software programs available for teachers and trainers who want to produce customized multimedia courses. Some of the most popular programs are Linkway, for IBM computers, and Hypercard and Course of Action for the Macintosh.

Authoring is not just for professional educators. It's a valuable skill for managers and supervisors in any environment where workers must periodically update their skills. It doesn't require an advanced degree. The basics of authoring can be learned in just a few courses.

A number of progressive colleges now offer state-of-the-art training in instructional technology, though others may lag behind. Asking a college education faculty about their course offerings in "authoring" is a good way to distinguish an up-and-coming institution from those that may still be wrestling with filmstrips.

Adapted Computer Technology

One of the other exciting arenas for instructional technology is the rapidly growing field of adapted computer technology: the use of computers to assist disabled people. Like many "new" inventions, ACT has actually been developing for a number of years. But in the past year or two, a whole array of computer-supported devices has suddenly come on-line.

While some of these devices are familiar to disabled clients, they've received a wave of new publicity since President George Bush signed the Americans With Disabilities Act into law in 1990. The ADA is a complex statute that revolves around three key phrases: "qualified individuals," "reasonable accommodations," and "undue hardship." In essence it states that no individual with the skills required to perform a given job should be prevented from doing so by a physical disability. The act requires employers to make reasonable modifications of work stations by acquiring the kinds of special equipment disabled employees may require, as long as they are able to do so without undue financial hardship.

Initial press coverage of the ADA has highlighted the work it will bring to architects, who will redesign facilities to accommodate the disabled, and attorneys, who will handle employee lawsuits.

The federal Equal Employment Opportunity Commission has estimated that ten to twelve thousand disability discrimination charges will be filed within the first year after the law goes into effect.

But in the long run the ADA may have a much greater impact on two other fields: industrial training and instructional technology. That's because, at the present time, an estimated two-thirds of America's forty-three million physically disabled citizens are unemployed. They're in a similar situation to citizens of the Two-Thirds World when it comes to mainstream economic life. Both groups are on the outside looking in. If either were to be incorporated in the larger economy, they would not just be job holders; they would contribute to the economy as consumers as well.

Today a whole range of adapted computer technology is available to assist disabled people in making that transition. There are computers equipped with speech synthesizers that echo every character entered from the keyboard and recite every word on the screen. They can enable blind people to work with computers. There are color-enhanced screen magnifiers for people with low vision, mouthpicks for quadriplegics, and telecommunications devices for the deaf that translate spoken words into written symbols.

The same development could occur with other devices, such as speech synthesizers. New technology could enable significantly greater numbers of disabled people to acquire marketable skills, which in turn could provide a market for bringing additional equipment on the market. It's a win-win cycle.

The signs of this revolution are already apparent. Paul Lorensen, who lost his sight to diabetes twelve years ago, teaches computer applications at the Colorado Center for the Blind. Lorensen instructs his blind students in state-of-the-art mainstream software such as WordPerfect and Lotus 1-2-3. He also works with individual blind clients on special career needs. When I spoke with him recently, he was trying to help a construction engineer who had lost his sight find software for estimating and scheduling building projects that could be adapted to voice synthesizers.

Lorensen is realistic about the challenges that blind people will continue to face in employment. He knows that new technology offers no panaceas. "Disabled people need to realize that there's no magic in computers," he says. "We still have to compete in the workplace. But computers can help us compete more effectively. And as I tell my students, if all else fails, you can always hire a pair of eyes at minimum wage!"

Updating Skills in Technical Professions

For people in high-tech fields, the process of staying current with changing technology is an unending challenge. That's because the technical environment in which they're employed is constantly changing.

Today the uncertainties that surround technical careers can be seen in a heated debate over whether America is running short of engineers. If there is a shortage, as some maintain, it's partly due to demographics. In 1985, as the last Baby Boomers were leaving college, seventy-seven thousand engineering degrees were awarded in the United States. By 1990 that figure had fallen to sixty-five thousand. From 1995 until the end of the century, there will be only fifty-six thousand grads per year. That's a decrease of 27 percent in only ten years.

The declining numbers have been even more evident in the case of women engineers, traditionally a small minority in the field. For a while in the 1970s and 1980s, as efforts were made to expand opportunities for women in the workplace, their numbers increased. Between the years of 1971 and 1987, the ranks of women engineering grads grew from 1 to 15 percent. But that was the heyday. Since then, their numbers have waned.

Add to that the fact that 75 percent of America's electrical engineering grads—one of the most vital fields for commercial research—have been going to work for defense contractors, and the problem looks worse. As economist Paul Harrington quips, "No wonder we can't come up with an $80 VCR!"

Talk with mid-career engineers, however, and you're apt to find a different view of the shortfall. When the engineering magazine *EDN* polled its readers recently, almost 80 percent said the shortage is a myth. "I've known quality individuals who took two years to find work," one manager said.

Perhaps the real truth is that what America lacks is not so much people with degrees in engineering as engineers with current skills. A couple of years ago I conducted a survey of training needs in a large, engineering-oriented corporation and found that the organization was struggling to implement a new concurrent engineering system. It was a method of using computer-aided design software to develop new products collaboratively, with specialists from several fields working simultaneously rather than step-by-step, as in the past. Concurrent engineering was vitally important to this corporation. All their competitors were using it to reduce costs and improve efficiency. As a result, they were losing bids on new contracts.

But the corporation I visited was unable to get its concurrent engineering program in operation. The reason was their workforce. They were stocked with middle-aged engineers who were uncomfortable working with computers, much less working concurrently with one another. When the company fell victim to defense industry cutbacks, it came as no surprise that those same mid-career engineers were among the first workers to lose their jobs. Some can be found today taking classes in computer-aided design at local technical schools: a good idea, but late in the game.

The moral of the story is one that turns up in many fields. While it's difficult to make any sort of broadscale predictions of future occupations in general, it is possible to spot patterns of change within a specific field. Usually, the first blush of change appears in retraining. In the case of engineering, several of the major professional organizations have good programs for assessing changing skills and identifying resources for retraining. One of the best is ESAP, the Engineering Skills Assessment Program, sponsored by IEEE, the Institute of Electrical and Electronics Engineers.

During the past decade, some good work-site continuing-education programs have appeared. Many are delivered via live television or video cassette recordings of lectures and technical demonstrations. That's important, given what's happening to the half-life of skills in the field of engineering. ("Half-life" in training refers to the time it takes for half of what one learned in school to become out of date.) In 1940 the half-life of engineering skills was about twelve years. Today it's only five years. In the case of software engineering, the half-life is something like three years. That's why IBM budgets four full working days of training for each of its technical employees every year.

High-Tech or Wide-Tech: the Generalist/Specialist Debate

Today, at some point in their careers, most technical professionals will face the important decision of whether to advance further in their specialties or to become generalists at the fringes of the high-tech arena.

One strong argument for generalizing is that most of today's new technical occupations are "wide-tech" jobs. Dale Parnell, who formerly headed the national organization of community colleges, coined that term to designate the application of high technology. Parnell believes that America's schools should give more attention to the use of computers in high-tech jobs, for example, than to the process of inventing new ones. Wide-tech jobs often combine technical skills with in-depth knowledge of a given industry. That's why a specialist in servicing computer systems for hotel operations will usually be recruited from the ranks of hotel managers rather than computer scientists: The primary requirement of the job is to understand the information needs of hotels that computers are intended to satisfy.

Many wide-tech jobs call for skills from more than one discipline or industry, unconventional combinations of technical and business skills. Electronic data processing auditors are an example. People in this fast-growing field must be competent in three fields: computer operations, financial analysis, and auditing. The skills are so diverse that, last time I checked, there was no academic degree program where one could learn them all. A recruiter told me that he looks for individuals who have strong skills in one or two areas and are motivated to learn the other skills on the job.

Wide-tech fields are jobs for generalists. High-tech fields are different. They may call for specialists with a graduate degree in one of the basic sciences. In the field of environmental consulting, for example, many idealists who majored in "Ecology" back in the early 1970s—the Earth Day era—are out of work today. As Ron Cohen, a geology professor at the Colorado School of Mines, puts it, "Today, if you call an ecology major at work, he answers with two words: 'Domino's Pizza!'"

Leonard Slosky, an environmental consultant, was an environmental activist who took a different path. Slosky began his involvement with the environment in 1970 when he founded Students Organized Against Pollution. It was a campaign against detergents that contained harmful phosphates. Slosky and his friends collected five thousand soap-box tops and mailed them with letters of protest to detergent manufacturers. The campaign was successful, part of a nationwide movement that helped to save Lake Erie. But then he attended to his own career future. He completed a master's degree in chemistry and was trained to perform the scientific analyses from which he earns a living today. "Science is a matter of many small steps," he says. "It calls for well-trained specialists. This is not a good field for generalists."

Still, I'm reminded of a physicist I saw as a career client last year. He was working in artificial intelligence, a field I'd researched for a newspaper column a few years ago. At that time there was a good deal of enthusiasm for the future of "knowledge engineers," who would become expert in synthesizing the operations of computers and the human brain as they developed "expert systems."

Now, however, my physicist-client said he wanted a career change. "What's wrong?" I asked him. "Don't you want to be a knowledge engineer?"

He snorted. "As far as I'm concerned, artificial intelligence has had its day. It's become just an academic exercise: a solution in search of a problem. I'm looking for a new field."

That's the risk we take in specialization.

In a society driven by technological invention, the generalist/specialist question will always be with us. Should we broaden our skills or focus our energies in a single field? High-tech or wide-tech: that's the perennial question for technologists.

Technology for the Rest of Us

For those of us who will never make a living from developing technology but will have to learn to use it in our work, I believe there's a set of skills emerging that might be described as "technical purchasing." It's simply the art of being an intelligent consumer of new technology. While I don't know of anyone offering courses in this field, I'll bet someone will in time. Here are a few items that might be included in a textbook on the subject.

One way to sharpen our skills as consumers of new technology is to consider the strategies manufacturers use to sell it. In the computer industry, marketing is a constant challenge. That's because computers, unlike, say, automobiles, can last a very long time.

Computer manufacturers have learned to segment their consumers into three groups: *the leading edge, advanced users,* and *followers.* The leading edge, sometimes referred to as "the leading, bleeding edge," represents high-tech innovators. These are the people who are fascinated by new machines. They'll buy the latest model of any device, just because it's new, often before the bugs are out of it. They're "technophiles." Manufacturers believe that the leading, bleeding edge constitutes about 10 percent of their market.

Advanced users, the second group, are more cautious consumers of new technology. They'll buy a new computer, but only after they've researched it in *Consumer Reports* to make sure the bugs are out. They're about 40 percent of the market.

The last half of the consumer market consists of followers. Some are "technophobes" who fear and resist machines of all types. The others are just reluctant to get on the bandwagon and try hard to make do with what they have.

In which category do you and I belong? That probably depends upon what we're trying to accomplish through a particular technology. Some analysts describe three uses of technology: basic, current, or pacing.

Basic technology is what we need to function in our jobs. A few years ago a typewriter was mandatory for anyone who had to do correspondence. Now, for many jobs, a computer and word processing are.

Current technology is necessary to stay competitive. In many information-intensive fields such as journalism, the ability to perform electronic searches of data bases is becoming part of that category.

Pacing technology is intended to put someone at the head of the pack. I know training consultants who always invest in the latest laser printer so that their materials will out-snazz everyone else's. Pacing technology is costly; it's for those who like to dance on the leading, bleeding edge.

If I were to choose an instructor for my course in technical purchasing, I'd look up a University of Houston professor named Christopher Dede. He wrote an entertaining article for school administrators which I picked up from some people at IBM. Here are a few of his pointers.

+ "Don't buy anything until you have determined why you want it. Beware of the temptation to give your organization a high-tech aura. Many of those devices will end up as expensive doorstops."

+ "Never believe something is available until you see it working. The three major kinds of instructional technology are hardware, software, and 'vaporware': a device program that is planned . . . anything you can't see or touch right now."

+ Recognize that "no single product or vendor is best for all situations. Power, cost, and ease of use are intrinsic tradeoffs; you can have any two of the three. For example, a powerful product with many functions will be difficult to learn and use unless the vendor has spent a fortune on development—then it will be expensive."

But Dede doesn't advise doing nothing. "Wisely chosen products are never obsolete," he says. And "never taking risks guarantees failure . . . living without risks is living dangerously."

Perhaps the important lesson is to ask good questions about the work we have to do and the resources available to us, then to upgrade our skills and equipment at our own best pace and time. I believe we'll see a growing market for consultants in instructional technology and technical purchasing, to help us all do that.

Resources

There are two well-recognized professional associations in the field of instructional technology. **The Association for the Development of Computer-Based Instructional Systems** is at 409 Miller Hall, Western Washington University, Bellingham, Washington 98225. Phone: (206) 676-2860. **The National Society for Performance and Instruction** is at 1126 Sixteenth Street, N.W., Suite 102, Washington, D.C. 20036. Phone: (202) 861-0777. Both groups sponsor annual conferences with extensive training programs. In addition, there's good training available from some of the principal manufacturers in the field. **IBM** has a training center in Atlanta. Phone: (404) 238-5689. **Bell Communications Research** sponsors seminars at its Bellcore Training and Education Center in Lisle, Illinois. Phone: (800) 832-2463.

The major meeting place for people interested in adapted computer technology is an annual conference entitled "**Closing the Gap**," which is held in Minneapolis each October. The conference is sponsored by an independent organization, also titled Closing the Gap. Their address is P.O. Box 68, Henderson, Minnesota 56044. Phone: (602) 341-8299. The organization also publishes a newsletter, whose title, as you might guess, is *Closing the Gap*. Subscriptions are $26 a year.

While currently there is no trade association for manufacturers and marketers of adapted computer technology, there are some good resources for users. **Job Opportunities for the Blind** is a data base with employment-related information. Phone: (800) 638-7518. **The Job Accommodations Network** is another resource. They're at (800) 526-7234. **The Adaptive Equipment Center**, another source of information, is at (800) 344-5405. The contact person is Ki Pisani.

For information on universities that offer continuing education in engineering, contact **AMCEE: the Association of Media-Based Education for Engineers**. Phone: (800) 338-9344.

One of the leading purveyors of advanced engineering courses in the workplace is **National Technological University** in Fort Collins, Colorado. Phone: (303) 484-6050.

Information on the **Institute of Electrical and Electronics Engineers' Engineering Skills Assessment Program** (ESAP) is available through IEEE. Phone: (202) 785-0017.

Christopher Dede's article, "Planning Guidelines for Emerging Instructional Technologies," appeared in the April 1989 issue of *Educational Technology Magazine*.

Chapter Sixteen

Telecommunications

In 1983, when federal Judge Harold Greene mandated the breakup of America's public telephone monopoly into eight component companies, he changed the economic landscape of the United States in a way few jurists have. The parent company, AT&T, was awarded the opportunity to manufacture telephone equipment and sell long-distance service. Seven regional phone companies were given the business of transmitting data—but not allowed to make equipment or generate the information they transmit.

The decision led to a course of legal maneuvering that continues to this day, as boundaries in the information industries are drawn and redrawn. Who will be authorized to create electronic information products, to manufacture devices for transmitting them, and sell the products? Telecommunications is an industry in revolution.

For each of the eight companies, "divestiture" was a call to re-invention. They had to come up with new ways of making a living, and fast. That process of adjustment is still underway. It's a difficult challenge for many employees, who had grown accustomed to the corporate culture of a public monopoly and assumed they'd be employed for life. Many of them are losing their jobs.

But for others, the rewards of telephone deregulation are enormous, as they are for the public at large. The telecommunications industry is producing a host of products and services that will radically affect the way most of us acquire information and communicate.

In this chapter we'll explore some of the changing skills and occupations in telecommunications—telecomputing, consultative sales, and data solutions. We'll also meet some interesting people who are inventing some exceptional new jobs.

✦ ✦ ✦

In Sterling, Colorado, a rustic town in the western plains, Dan and Laurie Jones are making high-tech history. The Joneses have founded a customer support and product testing service for computer software companies in the community where they grew up.

Dan Jones and Laurie Ganong were classmates at Sterling High School: class of 1971. They dated in high school but attended different colleges. When Dan graduated from Dartmouth in 1975, they married and moved to California. Both completed graduate degrees: Laurie an MBA and Dan a Ph.D. in physics.

Soon they had up-and-coming careers in Los Angeles. Laurie was with the Carnation Corporation and Dan with TRW. Work was good, but the Southern California lifestyle was horrendous. Commuting 15 miles to the office from their home in Redondo Beach could take an hour and a half.

Crime was everywhere. When Laurie went in to work one Labor Day and stopped to use an Automated Teller Machine on the way home, a gunman held her up and stole her car.

The Joneses decided to stop and take stock of their careers. Together they had fifteen years' experience in advanced technology and business operations, plus contacts all over the country. They suspected there were market opportunities for people with their skills in businesses that didn't require residence in Southern California.

That's when they came up with the idea of providing customer support services to software companies—from the town of Sterling, Colorado.

Software houses, like many high-tech firms, are notoriously poor at providing information to lay users. Often that's because they're too close to the products they've invented to understand the questions users ask. It's also because most technical professionals would rather work with machines than customers.

The Joneses judged that many software companies would be happy to outsource customer service: farm it out to a group of specialists. Suppose they were to train a fresh group of workers in customer service skills such as active listening skills, problem analysis, conflict resolution, and methods of instruction? They might employ the same staff to run tests of the software, as well. Beta-testing, the first test of products outside the laboratory, might be a complementary business. If they put that package of services together, could they move back home and run their business from Sterling? They both believed they could.

Today they have a small but growing company in a remodeled hardware store building in downtown Sterling. Commuting time:

four minutes. They recently sold the firm to Sykes Enterprises, a large computer-services company based in North Carolina. Through the sale they brought two hundred new jobs to Sterling while retaining top management positions for themselves.

Stories like that are surfacing all across the country, as "infopreneurs" (entrepreneurs who sell information services) recognize that their businesses can be conducted from almost anywhere at all. I know of a corporate consultant who leads seminars on information management coast to coast. He teaches clients to do information retrieval via computer modem and telephone line, allowing them to follow the Joneses' example—and conduct their business from their own home towns. The consultant lives in a town of 200 people.

Telecommuting

Telecommunications is making such lifestyles possible. But that's just for starters; we've yet to see the full impact of new work styles.

There's "telecommuting." The practice of working from home, transmitting data by computer modem and phone line, promises to relieve traffic congestion in crowded areas such as California. Currently, commuting accounts for an estimated half of all automobile use in California, and each year each car produces its own weight in carbon dioxide.

In Seattle, rush hours can last three hours, with traffic moving at an average of fourteen miles an hour. By the year 2000, the number of cars on the roads and highways of Seattle is expected to rise another 25 percent.

Telecommuting can take many of those cars off the road while reducing pollution and other traffic infrastructure costs, such as parking lots. It can also create new job opportunities for excluded workers, such as home-bound mothers and the disabled.

At last report, three and a half million Americans were working from home for outside employers. The total number of home-based workers, including the self-employed, is estimated at twenty million.

According to Marcia M. Kelly, author of an article in *The Futurist Magazine* (November/December, 1988), "The jobs well suited to telecommuting typically involve routine information handling, high telephone use, little face-to-face personal contact, a great deal of computer terminal work, and project-oriented activities with definite milestones. Prime occupations include computer programmers and systems analysts, lawyers, purchasing agents, accounting clerks, secretaries, clerical support, word processors, data entry clerks, insurance agents, accountants, and marketing managers." (From June

1990 publication of the Council of State Governments.)

Telecommuting requires two to three thousand dollars worth of special equipment—a computer with modem, and a telephone. Other components may include a fax machine, a networked computer system or electronic mail, teleconferencing equipment, and voice mail. Working from home also requires special qualities on the part of both employees and managers. Employees must be self-directed individuals with low needs for social interaction and reasonably happy home lives. Supervisors need to function as leaders and goal-setters rather than over-the-shoulder monitors. It's a transition easier to describe than to accomplish.

In recent years, social analysts have debated how widespread telecommuting is likely to become, given the social needs most of us meet in our work. That's why futurist John Naisbitt has criticized Alvin Toffler's notion of the "electronic cottage" as a model for the future. "Most of us aren't going to be content sitting home and tapping out messages to the office," he's said.

But other scenarios are emerging. Charles Handy, a British management consultant who grew up in Ireland, proposes that groups of telecommuters could spend their days working together, like the residents of the traditional village where he grew up. In fact, several "telebusiness work centers" are already in operation. They're located outside Honolulu, Seattle, Los Angeles, and Washington, D.C. The Hawaiian center, the Mililani Technology Park, opened in 1989. The facility employs seventeen workers. At last report there were three telebusiness centers in the Los Angeles area: at Apple Valley, Ontario, and Riverside.

Some employees work full-time at the centers, while others may spend only a day or two a week there; a respite from commuting and polluting the environment.

As the new work sites evolve, codes of conduct are beginning to appear. In the California facilities, guidelines specify that telecommuters dress in "business attire or dressy sportswear" while at the workcenter. Radios, televisions, and other personal entertainment equipment are not permitted.

There's an interesting parallel between the shifting trends in telecommuting workstyles, on the one hand, and the technology that makes those workstyles possible. It's the shift from large, structured systems, such as AT&T, to independent units, such as personal computers and telecommuters, to new forms of organization, such as networked computers and telebusiness centers. Most analysts believe that technology played an important role in the court decision to break up AT&T. The monopoly had been slow to introduce new devices to promote America's growing information economy. Now research is running full speed, and the telecommunications revolution is underway. As some commentators put it, we've gone from POTS to PANS: from Plain Old Telephone Service to Pretty Amazing New Stuff.

Still, it seems that the forces behind today's information revolution are not entirely technological. The leading entrepreneurs in this field appear to use advanced technology without becoming slavishly dependent on it. In fact many of today's most innovative enterprises run on generations-old technology.

The Wired City Committee

In Littleton, Colorado, economic development officials have developed an impressive array of programs to develop their local information industries. There's a software engineering institute, with courses transmitted over cable television, and an information-retrieval system for local businesses that transmits data from telephone lines to computers by modem.

It's the kind of avant-garde program one might expect to find in Littleton, a suburban community of engineers and computer scientists employed at the giant aerospace firm Martin Marietta. But, in fact, both the cable TV courses and information retrieval system operate over old phone and cable lines. In setting up both programs, the city formed a Wired City Committee to deal with the technical problems involved. They recruited all sorts of local "tekkies" to cobble together existing telephone, cable television, computer, and microwave devices for state-of-the-art information programs with no investment in additional telecommunications equipment.

It's the same case in Sterling, where Laurie and Dan Jones are running their software customer service business on old copper telephone lines and a fax machine—and nothing more in the way of twenty-first-century technology.

But when the next generation of technology takes hold, the growth in information industries could be explosive. Fiber optics technology has awesome capabilities for transmitting data: the entire contents of the Library of Congress, for example, in six seconds. Fiber optics systems are under development today in virtually every major American city. New York City, perhaps the information capital of the world, has a fiber optics network that stretches all the way to Princeton, New Jersey.

Home service is another matter. The best estimate is that it will be ten years before American homes have fiber optics linkage. But in the meantime, existing fiber optics networks and other ground communications systems are being connected with satellite transmission through new downlinking services called teleports. Satellites are the most powerful and cost efficient method of telecommunications. Each can handle a hundred thousand concurrent telephone conversations, together with three simultaneous TV signals.

There are currently thirty-five teleports in the United States, including one on Staten Island that connects nineteen orbiting satellites with the Manhattan-to-Princeton fiber optics cable system. As one of my associates commented the other day, "For the first hundred years of American history, industry developed alongside oceans and rivers. Then for the next 150 years it was built along railroads and airports. Now, it seems, the key to business development is having a good downlink."

The interim stage in telecommunications transmission is ISDN (Integrated Services Digital Network)—a common standard for converting analog sound waves into digital bits while using existing copper wire systems. It's a way to gain some of the benefits of transmitting voice, video, and data simultaneously—before the new fiber optics millennium really takes hold, around the turn of the century. ISDN technology has the capacity to help Laurie and Dan Jones, for example, to work with software customers visually, looking at their computer screens while they give advice over the phone and fax instructions.

That's the way telecommunications is evolving, toward integrated systems. The buzzwords among technicians in the industry are the "connectivity" and "interoperability" of all sorts of technologies in a day when the telephone dial has essentially become a computer key pad.

Today the technical skills required to work at the forefront of telecommunications are changing rapidly.

Mixed Skills

The growing integration of computers and telephone systems is creating strong demand for software engineers who are capable of designing and maintaining networks to meld the two. At present there are only eighteen university programs for software engineering worldwide.

It's a field with enormous potential both for individuals and for organizations that can manage their own software operations internally. Some of the most crucial challenges are the upgrading and integration of old software systems, maintaining the systems efficiently, and making software more modular.

Industries that are especially dependent on software include tourism, banking, retail and wholesale inventory and distribution systems, hospitals and other health care institutions, and telecommunications. In fact, any business with a large information base is a prime customer for software engineering skills. At US WEST, the Denver-based regional telecommunications company, software developers are being hired at a higher rate than telephone operators and equipment maintenance workers.

Much of the advanced work in the field involves interconnecting telephone and computer applications such as E Mail with programming in open architecture languages such as Unix and POSIX. The languages and acronyms change constantly in these "open systems" and "systems integration" functions. As one analyst told me recently, "telecomputing" is one field where you have to function as a specialist. But it's not like the old days in AT&T where you stayed in the same specialty all your life. A telecommunictions career today is an ongoing evolution of specialties.

In most cases, the best foundation for this process of continuous education is a good four-year college degree in electrical/electronics engineering.

Cellular Phones

One of the other exciting arenas of development is in wireless communication products such as cellular phones and paging devices. Cellular phones originated in the 1920s, when the city of Detroit installed a radio communication system in its police cars, but current technology dates from deregulation. According to the *Christian Science Monitor*, the numbers of cellular phones in use has increased from 230,000 in 1985 to almost 7.6 million in 1991. Despite that growth, the modern cellular industry is basically only six years old and accounts for less than one percent of all phone calls.

Cellular telephones represent the first efforts to commercialize the host of telecommunications products waiting to be marketed in the new economy. It's the first advanced telecommunications genie out of the bottle. That's significant, because in most sectors of telecommunications, most of the technical work in product development has already been done. From the French Minitel home information service to high-definition television (HDTV), there are all sorts of new products in the wings. What remains is to cultivate new markets.

Cellular phone systems are being pitched to both domestic and international consumers. Currently, domestic market penetration for all wireless products—basically cellular phones and pagers—is only about 6 percent. That market share is projected to reach 27 percent by the year 2000. But no one can be sure of the figure. That's because personal, ambulatory telecommunication is a new service. Motorola is banking on a steep rise in interest. They're constructing a satellite telecommunications system that will make it possible to link customers with small pocket phones all over the world.

But will telephone subscribers want that kind of service? One cellular phone official I spoke to believes that the technology will create its own demand. "We are in the process of determining standards for people everywhere as to how accessible they'll be," he told me.

Cellular companies are targeting their customers carefully. Who feels a need to be accessible at all hours? Who has problems with time management, struggling to return phone calls? Who works from multiple business sites? (That's the essential profile of wireless telephone system customers. So far, construction managers and physicians are prime targets.)

In some ways the international picture is more clear. Cellular technology offers a speedier, cheaper alternative to traditional landline systems. The cost savings range from one-third to one-half the cost of laying wires. In countries such as Mexico, that's an enormously significant statistic. Only 10 percent of residences in Mexico are wired for telephone service. Cellular systems are now under construction in many parts of Europe and Latin America, putting it in competition with Motorola's satellite system. But whichever system dominates, the benefits to developing countries are likely to be considerable. Studies in international economics suggest that telephone service is a leading factor in grasssroots economic development.

The culture of cellular phone companies is a night-and-day contrast to the old Bell system of regional phone companies which are still laying off workers steadily—workers whose skills no longer fit the new competitive conditions. Many of these people have the spirit of career officers in the military. They're accustomed to, if not dependent on, a structured work environment, and they feel lost in the new economy. But spend any time with cellular employees and you'll find an entirely different spirit. Most of these people are highly entrepreneurial.

Take Derek, a manager I know. Derek entered the field as a consumer. He'd been a regional sales representative for a farm implement firm, and the company had given him a cellular phone to use on his sales trips. The young man liked the phone so much, he joined the company. Now, five years later, he's been promoted eight times in a cellular firm that has grown from three employees to two hundred just in the past several years.

Like 50 percent of the employees in his company, Derek is enrolled in school. He's taking graduate courses in business. "In this business, people are only limited by themselves," he says.

Cellular telephone companies employ both technical and customer-service workers. Technical jobs may follow a somewhat predictable career path: from installer to programmer to repair technician for mobile phones to repair technician for portable phones. The basic skills are electronic. A two-year degree from a community college or vocational school offers good preparation. Related work experience, such as a repair technician job in a stereo shop, can be helpful too. The most specific training is in radio transmission technology. Those skills are often learned in the military or from one of the few trade schools that offer that kind of program.

In many telecommunications fields, the most sought-after technicians will have multi-disciplinary skills in electrical, electronic, and mechanical skills (for cellular phones, add radio transmission technology), plus the ability to communicate effectively with non-technical co-workers. Meanwhile, from all indications, the majority of jobs in cellular phones, as well as other telecommunications fields, will not be solely technical. Many will be in sales, since the primary need in the new fields will be to create demand and establish markets for new services.

Yet neither will these be solely sales jobs, as we commonly think of the term. Most new telecommunications jobs will require blended, hybrid skills. They'll call for unusual combinations of different kinds of abilities.

Sales and Service Jobs

Take the position of consultative sales. That's a term used by a regional telephone company that is hiring new staff at the same time it's downsizing. By "consultative sales" it means the ability to understand an organization's business and communication needs in order to create a customized package of products and services to meet those requirements.

The set of skills used in that process (which may take months or even years to culminate in a sale) is called "data solutions." The company is looking for employees who can make connections between telephone technology and business communications needs through innovative data solutions.

Obviously that's no small order. It suggests a complex of skills seldom found in a single degree program, skills in business operations, industry-needs analysis, interpersonal relations, verbal and written communication, and telecommunications technology. Add to that, for some, the ability to do in-depth analysis of a particular occupation or industry—the communications needs of physicians, for example.

In small organizations such as regional cellular phone offices, sales and marketing representatives also need a broad understanding of their company's internal operations. Frequently they must do most of the work involved in identifying new markets, recommending payment plans to clients, and compiling information for credit approval. Again, those are broad skills.

Most colleges are far behind the curve in offering courses and degree programs to help students acquire these hybrid skills. Compared to courses in computer science, telecommunications programs are hard to find. Some of the more progressive schools are beginning to develop "crossover courses" for technically trained people to bone up on business practices, and vice versa. But the need has scarcely been met.

One of the new spinoff occupations from telecommunications is telephone-based customer services. On-line service jobs are sometimes confused with telemarketing ("Hello, Mr. Smith? How are you? And how's your dinner?"). But they're similar only in working conditions. Both require that people remain stationary for long periods, connected to a phone and computer. Customer service people, though, are expert sources of information on their specialty—be it travel arrangements, health coverage, magazine subscriptions, or investment yields. The skills, again, are hybrid. They include data base searching, telephone etiquette, problem-solving, and sometimes stress management and sales.

Service representatives with health insurance companies, for instance, often deal with sick people whose problems of coverage may be a matter of life or death. Or take someone whose money order has been lost. Most people who buy money orders have insufficient funds for bank accounts. That's where stress management comes in. A lost money order is a major life crisis.

Most customer service positions, then, are a means of providing immediate information services to customers coping with complex data, using the capabilities of computers and phones. There are few formal training programs in on-line customer service. Most companies tend to hire people who have worked in some other service role and have basic familiarity with computers.

On-line information offices tend to cluster in mid-continent states where representatives can connect with customers from more than one time zone. In some places, working conditions are grim. Service reps may be monitored by computers that measure their efficiency in getting off the phone with customers as quickly as possible (that's called "talk time"). Even their disposition may be monitored ("tonality"). At one company, I'm told, thirty-nine service reps sit facing mirrors, so that they can make sure they're smiling as they talk with customers over the phone. To make matters worse, the mirrors evidently are monitored so that supervisors can check their expressions as well. It's no wonder that one of the best-selling books on the field is *The Electronic Sweatshop*.

But many teleservice offices are pleasant places, where turnover is low and wages aren't bad. Salaries in the mid- to high-$20,000 range are not uncommon. Customer service jobs may also offer mobility. They're often the entry-level "staging arena" for workers who may be promoted to other kinds of jobs. In an interconnected world with increasingly complex information needs and mounting data bases, on-line service is a sunrise field.

Professional Telephone Skills

Once again the nation's schools are lagging behind the curve when it comes to teaching new skills in business telecommunications. The other day I sat in on a half-day seminar presented by Career-Track, a private training company based in Boulder, Colorado.

Their ad for the Professional Telephone Skills seminar caught my eye because, like most Americans, I've found the number of calls I make is skyrocketing. I called Ray Boggs, a business analyst with BIS Strategic Decisions in Boston, to ask if he had any figures on the trend. He says that America's telephone bills are increasing at about 8 percent a year. That's twice as fast as inflation.

Boggs believes that much of the increase is due to business calls, which is what I'd sensed. It's clear that more and more business is being transacted by phone.

But it's not clear that we've all learned to communicate well that way. I know that I have problems closing off phone conversations. I find myself saying "bye-bye"—even if I'm talking with some big business honcho. It's a habit I picked up when my kids were small.

The audience at the CareerTrack seminar filled a good-sized motel banquet room. It consisted mostly of receptionists, customer service representatives, and telemarketers.

A lot of the program addressed receptionists' issues, such as what you tell a caller who wants to know why the person he called for isn't available. "Just stick to your role," the trainer advised. "It's not your responsibility to say why they're not at their desk—just that they're not there. Don't volunteer that, 'He's down the hall.' Or, 'Last time I saw him, he was headed down the hall, carrying a *Wall Street Journal.*' A simple, 'He's not available' will do."

Not all of that information spoke to my needs. But some of the telephone customer service skills were very relevant to bald, bearded professional types like me. For today it seems that customer service is becoming part of almost everybody's job.

I found several subjects intriguing.

On tone of voice: Research shows that in a typical telephone conversation, 16 percent of what we communicate comes from the words we speak, wile 84 percent comes from the way we speak. But telephone transmission reduces the amount of energy in our voices by 30 percent, so it's easy to come off sounding flat and indifferent.

That's why it's a good idea, when doing business by phone, to sit up straight and maximize your energy level. (That's also the rationale for General Electric's policy of watching their customer service reps smile into mirrors. Smiling improves articulation and bolsters one's energy level at the same time.)

On handling a non-stop talker. Try "bridging" the conversation back to the point of the call. Pick up a word from the caller's rambling monologue and transfer it to your own agenda. "Yes, speaking of 'working hard for your money,' Mrs. Fishbeek, I certainly have a pile of work right here on my desk . . ."

Another good technique is to match the speed of your caller. People speak anywhere from 150 to 350 words per minute. You'll connect better if you slow down or speed up to meet their cadence.

When dealing with an angry caller, try calling the person by name—though not necessarily their first name. The idea is to overcome alienation by establishing a relationship with the caller. Then you may be able to alienate the problem as something "out there" that both of you can work on.

According to CareerTrack, angry customers escalate through three stages. First there's disappointment: "The widget you sold me doesn't work." Then comes disillusionment: "And you seem unable to do much about it." Finally there's destructiveness: "Wait'll my lawyer gets hold of you!"

The idea is to cycle the customer back through those stages, to focus on the problem.

Innovations in Cable TV

Cable television is an industry with some serious marketing questions on its hands. It's a relatively new field. The idea of transmitting television signals by ground wire rather than airwaves originated back in the 1950s in the vacant plains of Wyoming. It was a time when oil exploration was expanding rapidly. Managers and technicians who had lived in large cities found themselves transferred to remote outposts such as Casper, Wyoming, where there wasn't a lot to do.

To make matters worse, they couldn't even watch television because the reception was so poor.

Before long, someone came up with the cable TV alternative, and a new industry was born. Technologically, cable was a smashing success. Within forty years, 85 percent of American homes were wired for cable reception. (By comparison, the telephone industry took a hundred years to cover the nation.)

So far so good. Except that currently only about 60 percent of homes across the United States that are wired for cable actually subscribe to the service. In some cities where service has been poor, market penetration is even lower than that.

Cable television has a problem. How can it attract more customers to use the available technology? One solution is to improve the quality of reception. That's what HDTV (high-definition television) is about. Soon there will be a concerted effort to sell new TV sets with motion-picture-quality reception.

Others in the industry are taking a different tack. Some note that the problems of marketing cable are similar to those in the personal computer field. PCs were introduced about 1973 and peaked within ten years. It seemed that consumers appreciated that personal computers were smart machines they could have in their homes; they just couldn't figure out what to do with them. By 1988 consumers were spending less for new computers than they were for software.

Cable television analysts watched both industries closely. They knew that about 20 percent of their cable subscribers owned personal computers, adding up to some eight million computers in all. Was there a way to connect the industries so as to create new products and add customers?

Taking a second look at cable technology, the analysts thought they saw a possibility in the addressable converter, a device that had been developed for add-on cable services such as HBO. It filtered special channels into households that paid an additional fee, and excluded the broadcasts from others. The technology behind the converter was found to have other uses as well. It was adapted to create the remote control device. And it also had the capability of connecting with personal computers.

To date, the cable TV and computer industries have yet to come up with joint products on a large scale. But there are some fascinating trial ventures underway. One of them is XPRESS Information Services, a joint venture that has been around since the mid-1980s. XPRESS transmits services such as newswire feeds through cable lines into personal computers. Customers, who pay about $100 for the necessary equipment but nothing thereafter, can receive stories from a dozen different wire services, filter them through combinations of a dozen key words, then read the stories on screen while deciding whether to run some off on hard copy or print them to disk.

It's an excellent service for people who want to follow events in distant parts of the world. Once, when my wife was on a project in Nicaragua at a tense time before the last elections in that country, I used the device to follow developments that weren't covered in the local press through a news wire in Mexico. At other times I've tracked scores from the Canadian Football League and political developments in East Africa—again, following stories on news wires that aren't covered locally.

Will XPRESS ever become a popular household product? It's hard to say. Thus far, their principal market has been schools. Students can use the device to follow course-related topics from different points of view—for example, comparing coverage of a story in China and Japan. The jury is still out on home information services, but a single successful new product could trigger an avalanche of job growth.

Rewiring Education

Meanwhile, another cable television company is pursuing a different sort of educational market. Four years ago, Jones Intercable launched Mind Extension University—a system for delivering formal education via television.

The program is the brainchild of Glenn Jones, an energetic entrepreneur who owns fourteen cable-related businesses. Jones has an obsessive interest in education. The first member of his family to graduate from college, he is convinced that many other Americans have an interest in bettering themselves, if they can overcome the logistical barriers to attending school. For working adults, home-bound parents, and others with full schedules, enrolling in a course can be a complicating commitment.

When he started his first cable television company in the late 1960s, Jones began to pay attention to the kinds of educational fare offered on TV. Those were the days of talking heads lecture courses and Sunrise Semesters, where students were forced to get up at 5:00 a.m. to study Spanish.

Prime-time educational TV was unfeasible, as the courses couldn't compete with commercial broadcasts. Jones considered many of the same questions that personal computer companies and XPRESS Information Service were to face. How can you market intellectual material to people in their homes—the environment where they expect to relax?

He knew that it would help if educational programming could be made more visually appealing and entertaining. That was one attack on the problem. But it didn't solve the scheduling problem; most adults were not interested in committing themselves to a regimen of watching televised courses. The solution turned up in a new invention: the video cassette recorder. Jones recognized that the VCR was revolutionizing the home entertainment field. People could now rent movies at their convenience rather than marching to the lockstep of TV and theater schedules. They could tape programs too. He recognized the potential of the VCR for education.

Jones began to track two trends in the cable television industry: the percentage of households that subscribed to cable service, and the percentage of people who owned VCRs. When both figures topped 50 percent, he began serious planning for Mind Extension University.

Today the Unversity enrolls thirty-six thousand students in one hundred courses each semester. The courses are supplied by twenty-one colleges and universities, plus organizations such as the Library of Congress. They broadcast high-school language and science courses during the day (Japanese, for example, to rural high schools that otherwise couldn't afford the subject) and courses for adults in the evening and at night. MBA students can set their video cassette recorders to pick up an accounting class broadcast at 3:00 a.m., then view it at their leisure.

Mind Extension is a case study in the benefits of strategic technical marketing. But the marketing challenge is ongoing. When I interviewed Heidi Byrne, a marketing manager for the company, she sighed, "Typically, when people decide to look into taking an accounting course, they don't automatically call their cable TV company. It's a new role for us. We're not just marketing anymore to people who want to know what time the fights are on."

Jones predicts that by the year 2000, seven million Americans will be enrolled in at least one distance education course, and that 80 percent of the nation's secondary schools will expand their curricula through television. He believes that distance learning will make education a major American export.

Like XPRESS Information Service, Mind Extension University is still not profitable. But it has begun to spin off new businesses. Last year, Jones Intercable produced a video disk on techniques for stringing TV cable. They're marketing the product to other cable television operators.

Meanwhile, Tony Amesa, a video specialist who once made his living filming weddings and bar mitzvahs, has begun producing TV courses instead.

"I realized I was running from one customer to another," he said in a newspaper interview. "It dawned on me I could produce something and years later continue to use it to teach people." Amesa has produced twelve tapes on computer literacy, which are broadcast widely. "I found I'm very good at simplifying complex issues," he says. "Video is a great teacher."

Stages of Invention

Telecommunications is a test case in the challenges of marketing new technology. Unlike ten years ago, when the problem was one of having too little technology, today there may be too much. That's certainly the case in cable TV, where consumers must be convinced they need an available product.

The industry also illustrates three stages in the use of new technologies. The first stage is *substitution*. People use the new device for activities they've pursued in the past. For example, when the automobile was first introduced, car owners simply drove to places where they had once traveled by horse and carriage. When the motion picture was invented, producers filmed stage plays.

The second stage is *expansion*. Car owners found they could go faster and farther by automobile, so they took more trips. In the case of cable TV, there's been a tendency to broadcast more and more basketball games.

Finally there is the third stage: *innovation*. Given the capabilities of the car, real estate developers came up with the ideas of suburbs, drive-in theaters, and shopping malls. The technology had created the elements of an entirely new economy.

Telecommunications today is just at that third juncture. Phone bills are rising; more business is being done over the telephone. At the same time, more information is being transmitted than ever before. As MIT researchers Thomas Malone and John Rockart point out, the fax machine is a stage-two device that enables people to do more and more of what they've already been doing—generating paper.

The real question when it comes to employment is, what will happen in stage three? That's why the early experiments in home information services are so significant. Those are new ventures into incredibly large potential markets.

The same process is occurring in telecommuting, where some of the work done in home offices is shifting to telebusiness centers—a new social invention.

That's why one of the most important new skills in technical fields may be technical marketing. It's no longer enough to invent new technology. Today the invention must meet a need and find a market. Technical marketing is a good subject for crossover courses. It's a subject that business and technical specialists in high-tech fields such as telecommunications would do well to study together.

Resources

The September 1991 issue of *Scientific American* ("Communications, Computers, and Networks") contains some exceptional articles on new developments in the field of telecommunications. I especially recommend "Computers, Networks and the Corporation" by Thomas W. Malone and John F. Rockart (page 128 ff).

Another good resource is *Data Communications*, a McGraw-Hill magazine that publishes an updated glossary of terms every year. For subscription information, call (212) 512-2699.

For those interested in learning more about telecommuting, contact **The Council of State Governments**, Iron Works Pike, P.O. Box 1910, Lexington, Kentucky 40578-1910. Phone: (606) 231-1939. Ask for a copy of their June 1990 *CSG Backgrounder*. It has an extensive bibiography of articles on the subject.

A related resource is *The Best Home Businesses for the 90s* by Paul and Sarah Edwards (Jeremy P. Tarcher Press, $10.95). The Edwards, whose interesting careers are described later in this book, are the authors of three other books on self-employment.

Another good book on independent living is *Country Bound! Trade Your Business Suit Blues for Blue Jean Dreams* by Marilyn and Tom Ross. The book is stocked with advice on how to develop a business in rural America while adjusting to the local culture. It's available from the Rosses c/o Communications Creativity, P.O. Box 909, Buena Vista, Colorado 81211. The price is $19.95.

For information on two suburban Los Angeles telebusiness facilities, contact **Dr. Sid Ward, Director: Telebusiness Workcenters, Inland Empire Economic Council,** One Lakeshore Centre, 3281 East Guasti Road, Suite 275, Ontario, California 91764.

For information on the Professional Telephone Skills seminar, call **CareerTrack** at (303) 447-2300. A recommended book is *Phone Power* by George R. Walther (Berkeley Books).

For information on **Jones' Mind Extension University,** call (303) 792-3111. Jones' book, *Make All America a School,* is published by and available from the company.

Chapter Seventeen

Tourism and Transportation

When the late futurist Herman Kahn predicted that tourism would be the world's leading industry by the end of the century, he had everything right but the date. By 1992, eight years short of the millennium, tourism was already number one.

Tourism is not only larger than Kahn anticipated; it's much more diverse than any futurist could have imagined. Tourism is a whole complex of industries, and it's tied to other fields, such as entertainment, education, aviation, airport operations, transportation management, materials management, and air cargo.

The best way to chart career opportunities in all these industries is to pay attention to skills that are emerging in three closely linked "T" fields: tourism, travel, and transportation. That's the aim of this chapter.

✦ ✦ ✦

Tourism offers more professions than meet the eye. Most of us are familiar with airline pilots and others whose jobs are highly visible. But many tourism jobs are in backroom operations. Get to know any of the major airports and you'll find several layers of subbasements where clusters of employees monitor traffic and baggage on computer screens. One airline I know of has 1,500 different job descriptions on file.

Part of the variety in tourism jobs stems from the fact that tourists are changing. Charter tour companies that once sent cast-of-thousands tours to trample historic sites are diversifying into niche markets such as ecotourism and Elderhostel. Some are seeking solitude and simplicity in their vacations. I know of one out-of-the-way region of Connecticut, the Housatonic Valley, where every fall, bed and breakfast lodges run ads with pictures of leaf rakes in the New York City newspapers.

"We sell stress reduction," their tourism director told me. "Lots of urbanites will come up here and pay for the experience of raking leaves. It's a way to recapture a simpler lifestyle."

Meanwhile, other tourists are seeking more stimulating experiences, as is evident in the burgeoning gambling industry that has overrun the United States since the 1980s. The key word is "experience." Tourism is an experience industry.

It begins with a destination: a place where people want to go. One of the basic tenets of tourism, as any industry professional will tell you, is that destinations change. Tourists don't always want to visit the same places.

Destination Marketing

That's why one of the most stimulating jobs in the industry is "destination marketing"—the business of cultivating tourist sites and selling them to the public.

Destination marketing is the art of capitalizing on tourists' interests in new experiences, to channel visitors into a specific country, state, or city. The profession, which began in the late nineteenth century with a salesman hired by some Detroit businessmen to promote their city, is now thriving at all three levels. According to industry analysts, whereas tourism is the third-largest industry in the United States, at state and local levels it often ranks number one or two.

Over a thousand municipal and metropolitan organizations sponsor destination marketing operations to tout local tourist attractions, hotels, and convention centers. It's a diverse field accommodating different philosophies. Some destination marketers specialize in tracking national trends, such as limited-stakes gambling. By bringing their communities into the mainstream of popular fads, they hope to generate new dollars from tourism. That's why, in the eighties, gambling spread like an oil slick from river cities in Iowa to the Black Hills of South Dakota to historic mountain towns in Colorado.

But faddist tourism has its drawbacks. By importing an attraction someone else has created, local workers often end up with low-paying jobs, while outsiders who control the industry profit. That's certainly true in the "gaming" industry, which has spawned hordes of minimum wage jobs. One study of the video lottery industry in South Dakota showed average annual salaries of $6,500 in bars and restaurants where the lottery games were played. Those were jobs for local residents. But the employees of firms that managed and serviced the video devices averaged $22,800 per year. Those were apt to be out-of-state workers. That's what comes from buying into someone else's fad.

Amusement and Theme Parks

Amusement parks are a one-time fad that seems to have matured into a national institution. Each year, according to the Travel Industry Association of America, 250 million people pass through the turnstiles of America's amusement parks. That's four times the attendance at major-league baseball games. Amusement parks are an enormous segment of the tourist industry.

According to the TIAA, the parks have changed significantly over time. In the early 1900s, amusement parks were a conglomeration of dance halls, swimming pools, restaurants, and picnic groves built near the edge of town, at the end of trolley lines. Some of these traditional parks are still going strong.

But with the advent of the automobile, a new kind of megapark evolved. Walt Disney introduced the theme park, with rides and special effects on a grand scale. Six Flags, Anheuser Busch, and other mega-park operators joined the fray. Today expenditures for capital improvements at the parks are soaring as they turn to an older clientele. In 1990, 80 percent of all visitors to Walt Disney World were over age eighteen. Nationwide, some 65 percent of amusement park visitors are eighteen or older.

Amusement parks are a major example of the growth in experience industries not only throughout America but worldwide. There's the new Disney theme park in France, and the underground city of York in England, where visitors can sample life in medieval times. There's also an impressive theme park in East Africa. In the Bomas (Swahili for "villages") outside Nairobi, Kenya, visitors can take in a two-hour performance by dancers and musicians from Kenyan tribal groups, then tour a reconstructed village, where "villagers" demonstrate crafts and sell their wares. Most of the patrons at the native performances are urban Kenyans with an interest in passing crafts and cultures. They're drawn to the Bomas for the same reasons Americans seek out bluegrass concerts.

While much of destination marketing involves basic advertising and promotional work, such as fielding phone calls, some of it is highly creative. The tourism professionals I met from the Housatonic Valley in Connecticut had developed a sophisticated strategy for marketing a region that had suffered many factory closings, and that otherwise might have received little notice. They represent a philosophy that's quite different from the business of following fads.

Local Tourism

Ned Book, president of the TIAA, has studied the skills involved in marketing local attractions. "Mostly it's cultivating an ability to see our surroundings with a fresh eye," he said. "It's taking an inventory of our resources and asking, 'What makes us different?' That's the way we discover the sites that could appeal to others."

Destination tourism is a great field for entrepreneurs with a kinky sense of humor and off-the-wall ideas for local attractions. Consider the Heeney Tick Festival.

The event began over a decade ago when a resident of Heeney, Colorado, a mountain town, contracted Rocky Mountain Spotted Tick Fever. The illness is no joke. It's no wonder that when the woman recovered, her friends decided to throw a big party. Somehow, things just took off from there. Today there's an annual parade, street dance, horseshoe tournament, and coronation of a Tick King and Tick Queen.

Then there's Bob the Bridge. When the town of Avon, Colorado, completed a new 150-foot bridge across the Eagle River, civic leaders thought the occasion called for more than a ribbon-cutting. They decided to name the bridge, and sponsored a local contest. The winning entry: just plain "Bob." The low-key moniker caught on, and 1992 saw a festival in honor of the bridge: BobFest '92, with a Bob-B-Que, Bobby Sox Party, Bob Ball . . . . You get the idea.

Tourism offers all sorts of opportunities for creative entrepreneurship. Thanks to such efforts, some of the most popular tourist destinations today are in places one would not necessarily expect. Can you guess which two states are the fastest-growing destination sites for foreign tourists? If you picked California as the number-one attraction, you're right.

But state number two? It's Kansas.

Certain kinds of tourists seem to be drawn to places that are just a bit off the beaten path, somewhat slower than life in the fast lane. Not long ago I sat in on a one-day course in understanding Japanese tourists. The Japanese represent a major sector of American tourism. In 1989, ten million of them traveled overseas, and half came to the U.S. They averaged eleven-day stays and spent about $4,000 apiece.

The class was led by a Japanese-American who was born in Tokyo and grew up on both sides of the Pacific. He offered some interesting insights into the motives of tourists from Tokyo, the city from which most of our Japanese visitors come.

"Imagine living in a city of twelve million people," he exclaimed. "Think of what it's like to drive there. Traffic is so dense that in order to own a car, you have to give evidence of a parking space. Parking fines are $500."

He told of coming upon a Japanese visitor to Colorado who had lagged behind his tour group as they entered a restaurant. The man stood behind the tour bus, gazing down the highway and across the open plains. He seemed to say, "Oh, if I could only get on that road and keep going!"

If empathy for foreign travelers is a valuable skill in tourism, so is appreciating one's own region. Most tourism specialists agree that one of the toughest challenges in their job is selling local residents on their own locale. When Missouri launched a tourism campaign a few years ago, it aimed most of its ads at its own citizens—trying to prime their interest in the state. As one marketer told me, "If people don't feel good about their own town, the first time they meet a tourist, they're apt to ask, 'What are you doing *here?*'"

For those with strong people skills who enjoy working with the public, several frontline tourism jobs are evolving. Lynette Hynings-Marshall, a veteran tour operator in Australia, opened a school to train tour guides in 1990. Tours are a big business in Australia, where 39 percent of the population travels abroad in any given year. Government subsidies and four-week vacations are designed to reduce the isolation of the island-nation through travel.

New Tourism Occupations

Hynings-Marshall offers training in three job roles: tour guides, tour managers, and international visitor specialists.

Tour guides are locally based specialists in a given region. They might live in Rapid City, South Dakota, for example, and specialize in the Black Hills. They take small groups of tourists on day trips. It's part-time, seasonal employment—the kind of work one might do as a second job, or in retirement. Guides are paid $8 to $12 an hour and may make twice that if they're bilingual. To find local employers, look for Tours: Operators and Promoters in the Yellow Pages.

Tour managers lead an altogether different lifestyle. They accompany groups of tourists on the road for wages of up to $150 a day, plus commission. It's a high-energy job, full of crises over misplaced luggage, canceled flights, and incompatible roommates.

Lynette Hynings-Marshall takes her students through role plays of problems with difficult clients, such as two lifelong friends who had never traveled together. Two days into a two-week tour, they're at each other's throats.

"Sit down with them over a meal," Lynette suggests, "and get them talking over old times—experiences they shared in childhood. Often that will help them become reconciled. But if all else fails, find them new roommates!"

Most tour managers are employed by large tour operations companies, such as Allied in Los Angeles, Globus Gateway in Denver, or Maupintour of Kansas. Check with local hotels to find tour companies that do business in your area.

The third job function, *international visitor specialist*, refers to in-house staff who cater to foreign associates of companies engaged in international trade. (It's an evolving role that may go by other titles, and it's usually an add-on skill rather than a full position.) As in the other roles, such specialists need to know a few words of greeting in the visitors' language, plus other cultural rules of thumb: don't pocket a Japanese business card, remember that Germans eat their salad after their entree, etc.

"The point is to get off the train of your own culture and onto the platform of another nation," says Hynings-Marshall. She advises anyone interested in travel and tourism to find his or her personal "customer service switch." That's the mechanism to turn on when one needs extra patience and energy for meeting the needs of others.

It's a familiar skill for anyone who's been around a service industry. My father spent his career in the transatlantic steamship industry, and occasionally conducted tours of Europe. Once when he was in a Swedish restaurant with a group of well-heeled and fastidious American widows, one of the women exclaimed over an especially tasty but unfamiliar dish. She called the waiter over to ask what it was.

My father signaled him to be evasive; he'd recognized the dish as horse meat.

Customer Service in Tourism

The American Society for Quality Control, a group that specializes in manufacturing, has begun to give concentrated attention to the service industries, where one-fourth of the membership is employed. They've circulated a stimulating article by a pair of French business consultants, Jacques Horovitz and Chan Cudennec-Poon: "Putting Service Quality into Gear" (published in *Quality Progress*, January 1991).

They recommend this strategy in a service organization:

✦ Take time to understand the needs of your clientele. A

European catering company wanted to improve the quality of its service at airport bars and restaurants. By surveying customers, they found they were serving two groups: (a) travelers hurrying to catch a flight who had limited time; and (b) those with time to kill, who didn't care about speedy service. While the two groups had somewhat different needs, both wanted a comfortable lounge where they could unwind.

✦ Be sure that you and your employees have a common understanding of quality service. Is it a priority to refill coffee cups every ten minutes? Many organizations are becoming more and more explicit about customer-service procedures. At Disney World there are written guidelines on how to take tickets at the gate. Written instructions always must be supplemented by hands-on training.

✦ Provide plenty of support to frontline service staff. They're your internal customers. Care for them much as you would want your customers to be treated. Don't be afraid to roll up your sleeves and join them in the trenches.

The Outlook in Lodging

One of the largest hospitality fields is lodging. It's a sixty-billion-dollar industry with forty-five thousand establishments and three million rooms. It is also one of the world's most accessible industries. Hotels have an abundance of entry-level positions.

Like many travel and tourism operations, the lodging business has been notoriously unstable. Hotels overbuilt during the 1980s. During the past several years, occupancies have declined, along with financing for new construction. As a result, it is anticipated that hotels will compete increasingly through guest services.

That's good news for career changers. Hotels, like other service providers, value the social maturity that usually comes with age.

Hotels come in several different species, distinguished by their rates and the kinds of services they offer.

Budget hotels offer no-frills accommodations for $30 a night or less, with no pool, bar, or restaurant. *Economy hotels* include these amenities for $50 a night. Together, budget and economy hotels make up almost 40 percent of the lodging market.

Upscale hotels range in price from $45 a night to out-of-sight. In return, they offer additional conveniences that may include twenty-four-hour front-desk and room service, concierge service, and health clubs. Classy hotels at this level are heavily dependent on income from banquets and conferences.

A new wrinkle in recent years is the *all-suite hotel*, which offers separate living and sleeping quarters, kitchen facilities, and most of the comforts of home to long-term business travelers. Rates range up to $150 per night.

Resort hotels are similar in price to the upscale variety, with even more emphasis on conferencing. Most resorts employ professional meeting planners, who attend to logistical details. The relationship of resort employees to their guests is more involving than in overnight hotels, since the guests are in residence twenty-four hours a day—sometimes for a week or two at a time. Often there are programs for families.

When it comes to employment, hotel jobs can be found in three arenas: rooms, food and beverage service, and administrative support. In a typical lodging facility, 60 percent of the jobs are relatively unskilled.

Most entry-level jobs pay minimum wages, but some may be more profitable than others. In a restaurant, those who provide direct service to customers—waiters and waitresses, for example—may earn several times their hourly wage in tips. Hostesses, in an apparently more attractive position, typically earn much less. The same is true in hotels. Front-desk jobs may appear more desirable than cleaning rooms, but housekeepers may make almost as much as clerks.

Of course, the truly profitable jobs in lodging are all at the top. Managers typically make $60,000 a year. The hours are long, however, and crises are common. Guests have heart attacks, computers malfunction, and employees are always coming and going. Hospitality is a stressful business.

I once had a young career counselee with a hotel/restaurant degree who decided to change fields after spending several years in country club management.

"Why the change?" I asked him.

It turned out that he'd recently married and had given some fresh thought to his career. As he reflected on the successful country club managers he knew, it occurred to him that every one of them was divorced.

Still, if there are hazards in the hospitality industry, there also are opportunities. Hotels are one of the last remaining pyramid organizations, with lots of entry-level positions at the bottom and on-the-job training most of the way to the top. Even those who study hotel/restaurant management in college must pay their dues in entry-level jobs. In fact, a typical college HRM program will require a thousand hours in internships (read: making beds, slinging hash). That's because managers in the hospitality field must be able to perform every job in their institution on a moment's notice. With low-wage jobs and low-skill workers, employee turnover may average 200 percent a year. Some ski resort restaurants suffer a 230 percent turnover in staff during every six-month season.

Needless to say, the hospitality industries are expert in on-the-job training. One of the newest wrinkles is to combine video courses with in-house trainers. Some professional lodging associations offer a sequence of courses with certificates for each level. That's beneficial for employees who may want to transfer their skills from one organization to another.

In addition to working one's way up the organization in a conventional hotel, there's another career path to consider. Many Americans of "early retirement age" (which in this day of corporate layoffs can mean almost anyone age forty-five or older) are cultivating new careers in resort communities. You can find these individuals in almost every attractive region of the United States. They're drawn to places they've visited as tourists, often to pursue lifelong interests such as skiing. In a society where the "birth dearth" has drained the traditional labor pool of young adults, resorts have been turning to older workers. It's a natural match for energetic career changers who are years from traditional retirement.

Here are a few typical stories from ski resort towns in Colorado.

Bud and Jeanne Morrison

The SCOTTY'S BAR-B-Q sign appeared through misting snow down a side street of Steamboat Springs. It was early evening in February, and the temperature was falling faster than the sun. Scrambling in out of the cold, I found myself in a small wood-paneled bar with a warm fireplace and the pungent scents of hickory smoke and barbecue sauce.

At five o'clock, the place was packed. I took the last table, near the door. The barbecue at Scotty's was so good, I had two plates of ribs. I asked about buying a bottle of sauce to take home. Soon I was talking with the owners of the place, Bud and Jeanne Morrison.

It seemed they'd discovered Steamboat Springs while driving from their home in California to visit friends in Denver. The Morrisons enjoyed driving through the mountains, and enjoyed the old ranching town of Steamboat Springs in particular. It was the kind of place where they'd dreamed of settling.

Bud had put in seventeen years with Chevron in the Bay area, commuting two hours each day to work. There was talk of an early retirement program at the oil company. At age forty-three, he was ready for a change. The next time the Morrisons drove to Denver, they stopped to see a real estate agent about homes and businesses for sale. That's how they found Scotty's.

Carl Scott had grown up with the barbecue business in Texas. He'd been operating Scotty's in Steamboat for ten years or so and had enjoyed experimenting with new recipes—combining the woods of local fruit trees with the traditional hickory. But now he was ready to retire.

The Morrisons negotiated an agreement to purchase the restaurant, with a special clause. Scott would stay for two months to teach them the business. Happily, the new owners caught on quickly. Today their lives are full of the barbecue business. They try out new recipes on local residents during the off-season and enjoy their small-town life year-round.

Bob Flint

Bob Flint was sixty-seven when I met him in Breckenridge. He'd been retired in the Summit County ski town for ten years. Flint had spent thirty-five years as an electrical utilities engineer for Commonwealth Edison, a public utilities company in Illinois. It was a stressful job, full of midnight emergencies. The one thing he enjoyed about the company was its annual employees' ski trip to Colorado.

One day Bob came home from work with a packet of information on an early retirement offer. As he walked in the door, he asked his wife, "How about moving to Colorado and becoming ski bums?"

She said, "When?"

Nowadays Flint works three days a week in the visitors' center at the edge of town, and skis the other days. He looks ten years younger than his age. "I'm probably still alive because of this move," he told me.

Anita Starzer

Anita Starzer lost her job as an oil and gas accountant when the energy industry crashed in the late 1980s. The odds against finding another accounting job in Denver seemed astronomical. A CPA she knew had enrolled in a truck driving school. One accounting ad in the Sunday newspaper drew seven hundred applicants. Somehow, she decided, she had to expand her market.

Leafing through job notices one day at the public employment center, she saw an opening for an accountant at a ski resort. When she called, it was filled. But then she began calling other resorts, town by town, in the mountains. Each time, she asked to speak to the controller.

On her twentieth call, she finally connected with an opportunity. When she asked for the controller at the Holiday Inn in Vail, the receptionist told her, "We don't have one." Starzer drove up to Vail and asked the motel manager what he needed in the way of financial management. He gave her a part-time job in accounts receivable.

Two years later I interviewed her in the sunlit dining room of the Holiday Inn at Vail on a gorgeous Saturday morning in September. The aspen were turning color and the whole town was shimmering in gold.

Starzer's career seemed to be thriving. During her first two years in Vail, she had been promoted from part-time accountant to controller and then to director of personnel. That's not to say that her life was without challenges. Like most mountain workers, she was spending about 40 percent of her income on housing: renting a townhouse while subleasing bedrooms to fellow employees, trying to reduce the rent. It's not a lifestyle everyone could manage. But visiting with her that morning in September, it was hard to miss the sparkle in her eyes and the sense of new life. Her career was on the upswing again.

By now, you probably sense some of the basic rules of thumb for finding work in resort communities. Here's a brief recap:

1. Visit the site in which you have an interest, early and often—and in all seasons of the year. It's not enough to have visited the place as a tourist. Discover how hot the place gets in the summertime, or what the muddy season is like. Try to find out what you're in for.

2. Do your homework on prospective employers. Don't assume, for example, that an attractive resort has desirable working conditions. I've interviewed a number of ski-resort employers while researching my newspaper columns. In one instance I found the personnel director at one of Colorado's classiest resorts extremely cold and guarded, unwilling to tell me much about her staff. The next winter a Denver tabloid newspaper ran an expose on "acquaintance rape" in the resort's employee dormitory. It seems that the resort had put up the dorm ten years ago when young adults, the traditional ski resort employees, were in good supply. Now the ranks of

young adults are thinning. But the resort continues trying to hire in that age group because it needs single adults to fill the dorm. As a result, they're scraping the bottom of the labor pool and recruiting acquaintance rapists.

Reading the story, I knew why the personnel director had been reluctant to talk with me. It's an example of the need for good background information.

3. Always contact tourism employers directly—by phone or in person. Hospitality industries are a "now" business where professionals are accustomed to making quick decisions. They're also a business based on personalities. Let them respond to yours, and be prepared for a quick decision.

4. The best time to move to most resort communities is six months ahead of tourist season. When you find a good job in the place you want to be, don't sign on until you've taken care of housing. For ski resorts, that means looking in April rather than October.

Come Fly Away

Is there anyone who hasn't dreamt of turning in a tedious job for a glamorous career with the airlines? Realistic or not, most of us harbor fantasies that aviation is a plenty exciting way to make a living. Actually, most airline employees I know do love their jobs. In one airport, two-thirds of the ticket counter customer service reps have been there fifteen years or longer. "Once you're in this environment, it's hard to go back to an office job," their supervisor observed.

Airlines are a great field for people who thrive on stimulation: the challenge of a job where every day is different. But the downside of the industry is that stimulation seems to have escalated into anxiety over unemployment. The industry is notoriously unstable. Since deregulation in 1982, airlines have downsized to curtail costs. United Airlines, in 1982, operated at 96 percent of its capacity in 1978, but with 21 percent fewer workers. Unfortunately, cost cutting hasn't brought stability. Since 1982, 104 new airlines have been founded and 104 have failed. During the Persian Gulf War, when fuel prices doubled, three American airlines went out of business and three others filed for bankruptcy.

Still, the industry is growing in every sector by an average of 3 to 5 percent a year. One of the fastest-growing sectors is air cargo: shipping and distributing personal packages and manufacturing components. Another is international travel. Transatlantic flights are increasing at 7 percent a year and transpacific flights even faster.

Out of the turbulent growth, it seems that the American aviation industry is separating into two segments. Most analysts expect
that when the takeover/merger dust clears, there will be three global
mega-carriers (American, Delta, and United) and a complex of
smaller airlines serving local regions and other niche markets.

Job opportunities vary. Some of the highly skilled positions—
pilots, air traffic controllers, and mechanics—offer good opportunities for those who are open to long-term training. The market for
aviation mechanics, who train for two years before taking a Federal
Aviation Administration exam, is expected to increase 5 percent a
year for the foreseeable future. Those are good, professional positions with an average salary of $45,000 a year.

Career changers who may not be mechanically inclined, or
open to two years' training, may find opportunities in customer service. Like 95 percent of airline jobs, the work does not require a college degree. But it does call for exceptional personal qualities.

I spent part of a working shift with Mick Evans, a United Airlines customer service rep, not long ago. Evans is a calm, congenial
fellow in his fifties who has been in the field for thirty years. He began his career in a small airport in Akron, Ohio, doing everything
from handling baggage to calculating fuel supplies to cleaning air-
planes. Most professionals in aviation recommend starting out in a
small facility because of the broad duties and learning opportunities
available. I stood by Evans' counter for half an hour, listening to a
stream of passengers' questions:

"Is it too late to upgrade to first class?"

"What's the weather like in Sioux City?"

Suddenly three young women came running up to the counter.
One of them was carrying a baby, and she was in tears. They wanted
to report an off-duty pilot who, they said, had cursed at them for
standing on the wrong side of a moving walkway. He'd snarled, "Get
out of my way! Can't you see I'm a captain?"

The customer service rep took time to get all the details of the
story, then worked on identifying the pilot and filing a report. It was
stressful work. If guilty, the pilot would receive a reprimand. If it
were a second offence, he could lose his job.

Stress management is a basic skill for Evans' position. But so is
information management. Customer service reps undergo a constant
round of training, both in classes and in a weekly update of fare and
schedule information that comes up on their computers. Fifteen
years ago, computers were unknown to the job. Seat reservations
were marked with gummy labels on cabin charts. Today it's hard to

imagine a profession with sharper keyboarding skills than those of the airline counter people. United Airlines retrained several hundred Denver customer-service representatives in computers—keyboarding plus data base searching—without losing a one. Career paths are fairly clear. Employees are usually hired from another service industry, such as a travel agency. After initial training, they're assigned to one of the counters at the front of the terminal. Only when thoroughly trained are they moved to the gate. Salaries are low at the outset, but an experienced customer service rep can earn well over $30,000 a year, plus travel benefits that may include one's entire family.

It's a tough but interesting job. As Richard Ferris, former president of United Airlines, once commented, "Travelers are not tolerant." He might have added, tourists can be terrorizing. "Especially in ski season, when they come racing down the mountains, late for their plane," says Evans, "it's great work, if you like variety. Every day is different."

Here is a summary of some typical entry-level jobs within United Airlines. Salaries are for beginning workers as of April 1992.

Customer Service Representative ($1,250.00/month). These employees deal directly with customers at airport locations. Duties at major airports involve answering questions on schedules, fares, and aircraft; handling service irregularities; and processing minor claim settlements. Representatives at smaller stations perform additional duties that may include baggage and cargo handling, dispatching of aircraft, air freight sales and service, and others.

Reservations Sales Representatives ($1,210.00/month). These employees answer telephone inquiries regarding fares, schedules, and special services, and make reservations for air travel tours, car rentals, and hotel reservations. The environment is computer-oriented, and the emphasis is on producing sales.

Ramp Service Employees ($9.03/hour). Their work consists of loading and unloading cargo, mail freight, baggage, and food services supplies from airplanes. It requires the ability to operate a variety of motorized equipment and to use sophisticated baggage equipment.

Food Service Employees ($6.49/hour). These individuals are responsible for the cleaning of flight kitchen utensils, equipment, and facilities. They also operate dishwashing and packaging equipment. Duties include setting up meal trays and preparation of salads, sandwiches, and other cold dishes.

Cabin Service Employees ($6.93/hour). These employees perform cabin cleaning and supply setup, as well as lavatory tank servicing on all kinds of aircraft. They also collect and remove trash from passenger, cockpit, and galley areas, empty trash containers and ashtrays, and sweep and vacuum floors.

As you can see, we've covered some ground in this section—from glamorous jobs to the basic nitty-gritty. It's important to remember the entire spectrum when we think of job growth in transportation and tourism. Many of the jobs are in out-of-the-way occupations. But they're not all mundane, and some of the jobs pay well.

Transportation Arrangers

Take transportation logistics. The field may not be a household word, but it's growing steadily across the United States.

Transporation managers carry any number of titles, from materials manager to inventory and warehouse manager to transportation logistician. In each case the duties are similar. Transportation management is the business of moving and distributing material supplies and packaged goods by air, water, highway, or rail. Someday the list will include space.

The skills required to manage transportation are like those in other logistical operations: verbal and written communication, negotiation, computation, computer applications, and business law. They're not unlike skills one finds in the military. But the pay is considerably better in the private sector. Mid-level managers commonly earn salaries of $30,000 to $40,000 per year.

Jobs are plentiful, since about 20 percent of the Gross National Product in most societies comes from transportation. In the United States the transportation sector accounts for something like 10 percent of all jobs, and the share is growing.

In the case of the burgeoning air freight business, growth is being fed by two factors: a lack of confidence in the federal postal system, and a growing sense that lots of items "absolutely, positively have to get there overnight."

Just-in-time manufacturing is another contributing factor. Companies have begun to realize enormous savings from ordering supplies on the spot rather than keeping vast inventories on hand. Anthony Carnevale's book *America and the New Economy* documents a number of examples. A motorcycle manufacturer cut production time from thirty days to three while reducing costs by half. A computer manufacturer used a just-in-time system to reduce inventory by 60 percent, space requirements by 30 percent, and labor costs by 20 percent.

In other fields, similar gains are waiting to be realized.

Carnevale cites a recent study of the apparel industry, where it ordinarily takes sixty-five weeks to convert raw material to a finished product. It seems the material is being worked on only fifteen of those weeks. Analysts estimate that manufacturing costs could be shaved by 25 percent if efficiency were improved. Transportation is part of the solution to that sort of problem.

Another growth factor in transportation management is increased global trade. Today manufacturers with specialized products need to connect with customers in niche markets all over the world. A recent survey of up-and-coming companies in Colorado found firms selling products overseas ranging from Healthy Kleaner (a surgical tape and bandage remover) to a twisted wire designed for opening pistachio nuts. Mark Zirinsky, a young inventor, has brought twenty products to market. His biggest seller is a device called Power Trip, which enables computer-users to draw on a power supply through the cigarette lighters in their cars. The kinds of go-go business people who would buy such a device are found world-wide, and modern transportation is the key to reaching them.

Zirinsky's Power Trip is currently sold in thirty-four countries, and 40 percent of his total sales are overseas. Multiply that story by all the niche-market entrepreneurs in the global economy, and it's clear why transportation logistics is a growing field. But why isn't it better known? One reason may be that it's a back-office business. Working out the details of a parts shipment doesn't carry the glamor of piloting an airplane or the visibility of serving as a travel agent or a conductor on a train. Then, too, transportation management has not relied extensively on formal training. Talk with people in the field, and you'll find that most of them simply fell into it. It was a summer job or a position that unexpectedly came open in their organization.

That pattern is changing today, as community colleges in particular offer new courses and degree programs. Most programs include instructors who are practitioners in the field and offer internship opportunities. For information, call local colleges and ask for information on programs in transportation logistics or transportation management.

The Open Road

Finally there's truck driving. Yes, truck driving.

I became interested in the field when I was giving a talk to a group of transportation managers—commenting, as I often do, on the changing American workplace and wondering what we're to do

with our zillions of displaced white-collar professionals in America.
"What about trucking?" asked one of the transporters. "Most
of us are hurting for good drivers."

I did some research and learned that trucking has been an industry in transition since former President Jimmy Carter signed the
Motor Carrier Act into law back in 1980. Since then, major trucking
lines have consolidated, with the loss of many jobs.

At the same time, thousands of independent operators have
gone out on the road. Conditions are still so chaotic that no one is
sure how many of these independent truckers there are, nor how
many are employed in the industry at large. The U.S. Department
of Commerce quotes estimates anywhere from 3.5 million to 8 million trucking employees in the nation.

The labor shortage seems to have been sparked by efforts on
the part of the federal government to restore some order to this
chaos. There have been concerns about highway safety. Last year
the government introduced a standard Commerical Drivers License
exam with a series of rigorous written tests. There also has been
more aggressive drug testing.

For the past few years, large truckers such as Werner Enterprises in Omaha have been hiring more mid-career drivers in their
thirties, forties, and fifties. Some are married couples. Many are military veterans with experience as truck drivers or heavy equipment
operators. In those cases, the company often provides in-house
training to build on the veterans' existing skills. Others without experience, like Anita Starzer's CPA friend, enroll in professional
schools of truck driving. Here the watchword is, watch out. In recent
years, truck driving schools have been regulated as loosely as the
rest of the industry. A number, in fact, have run afoul of the federal
government over unpaid student loans. Some say the reason those
loans have gone unpaid is that students who took them out are unemployed, having received poor training.

For all those liabilities, there are some interesting rewards in
the field. Salaries aren't bad, for one thing. An efficient driver with
several years' experience and a good safety record can make over
$30,000 a year.

More than that, there's the lifestyle. Out at Coors they tell the
story of a fifty-year-old secretary who quit her job a few years ago to
become a truck driver. Was it a good career move? No one is sure.
They haven't heard from her since. Trucking is like that. It's a vaga-
bond profession that appeals to people with a footloose lifestyle.
That's especially true of TL or "truck-load capacity" drivers. Those

are the people who often have long layovers in distant cities while they wait for a full load to haul back home. It's a business of unpredictable schedules.

LTL or "less than load" drivers have a much more stable lifestyle, working local routes. They're home more often. But the trade-off is driving boring routes—out on the local interstate today, back tomorrow, and out on the same interstate the day after. One transportation manager told me he'd established a career path and reward system for his truckers. So many years as a TL driver, and you'd get an LTL route so that you could be home every evening. To his surprise, several of the drivers who qualified for the prize routes came to him after a month and turned them in. They missed the excitement of the long haul and the open road.

He said, "That's when I realized truckers are basically professional tourists."

Resources

For information on destination marketing, contact these organizations. At the national level, **United States Travel and Tourism Administration**, U.S. Department of Commerce, Washington, D.C. 20230. Phone: (202) 377-0137.

At the state level, the **National Council of State Travel Directors**, c/o Travel Industry Association of America, is at 1133 21st Street, N.W., Washington, D.C. 20036-3390. Phone: (202) 293-1433. Or contact the travel and tourism office of your state.

For marketing individual cities or local areas, contact the **International Association of Convention and Visitors Bureaus**, P.O. Box 758, Champaign, Illinois 61824-0758. Phone: (217) 359-8881.

Leaf through the Sunday travel section of any major newspaper, and you'll find a trove of promotional tourism ideas. Some tourist programs have social significance, such as travel to Vietnam. There are **SeaQuest Cruises** (1-800-854-8999), and land tours by **Abercrombie & Kent** (1-800-323-7308) offer Vietnam excursions.

Then there's **Elderhostel**, an education/recreational program for adventurous older Americans. The program, founded in 1975 by an educator in New Hampshire, is based on European youth hostels and Scandinavian folk schools for elders. It provides short-term courses, mostly in the summer on vacant college campuses, for people over sixty.

By melding the rising trends of experience industries and an aging population, Elderhostel has established a major niche in the new economy. In its first eighteen years, more than two hundred thousand senior citizens have participated in the program. Today courses are offered at sixteen hundred locations in the United States and forty-three other countries. **Interhostel**, a new adjunct to Elderhostel, sponsors the overseas study programs.

Recently, the Elderhostel program has spawned yet another new tourism offering: **Familyhostel**. The program provides overseas educational and vacation experiences for children, parents, and grandparents traveling together.

For information on **Elderhostel**, contact the organization at 75 Federal Street, Boston, Massachusetts 02110-1941. Phone: (617) 426-7788. For **Interhostel** and **Familyhostel**, contact the University of New Hampshire, 6 Garrison Avenue, Durham, New Hampshire 03824. Phone: (800) SEE-WRLD (733-9753).

For the physically active and socially concerned, there is **Habitat for Humanity**, an ecumenical Christian organization that helps indigent people construct housing. The program was founded in 1976. Today it sponsors housing construction projects in twenty-seven countries and at a number of sites across the United States. Habitat is an ideal activity for religious organizations interested in building relationships among members through ventures in social service. As a travel and tourism enterprise, it's like Elderhostel—a way of offering meaningful experiences to people who want to do something constructive with their leisure. For information, write to **Habitat for Humanity International** at Habitat and Church Streets, Americus, Georgia 31709-3498. Phone: (912) 924-6935.

Other tourism-with-purpose programs are springing up around the country. One is the **Consortium for Community-Centered Comprehensive Child Care**: C-6 for short. The program provides medical assistance to children of the Masai tribe in northern Tanzania, a region founder Jim Buchanan toured in 1984 when he went to East Africa to visit a client. Buchanan was impressed by the suffering among the Masai, a nomadic tribe vulnerable to Western diseases such as measles and tuberculosis. An estimated one-third of Masai children die before the age of five. Buchanan blended tourism with social service by enrolling Americans in expeditions to climb Mount Kilimanjaro in Tanzania. Participants recruit sponsors, who pledge $10,000 to support their climb. Thus far, the project has raised more than $700,000 to construct hospital buildings and support medical education in Tanzania. For information, call Heather Fleck at C-6: (303) 595-4331.

For those recovering from alcohol and drug addictions, there's

Recovery Adventures, P.O. Box 1377, Brookline, Massachusetts 02146. Phone: (617) 323-7511. For listings of companies that sponsor similar excursions, contact **Sober Times**, P.O. Box 40259, San Diego, California 92164. Phone: 1-800-882-3303.

For information on association-sponsored training programs in lodging, as well as other developments in tourism, contact the **Travel Industry Association of America** at (202) 293-1433.

These are some other associations in the field.

The American Hotel and Motel Association, P.O. Box 1240, East Lansing, Michigan 20005.

The Air Transport Association of America, 1709 New York Avenue, N.W., Washington, D.C. 20006.

The Air Line Employees Association, 5600 South Central Avenue, Chicago, Illinois 60638.

The American Society of Travel Agents, 1101 King Street, Alexandria, Virginia 22314.

The Institute of Certified Travel Agents, 148 Lindon Street, P.O. Box 82-56, Wellesley, Massachusetts 02181. Phone: (800) 542-4282.

The Regional Airlines Association, 1101 Connecticut Avenue, N.W., Washington, D.C. 20036.

For further information on transportation management, contact **Delta Nu Alpha Transportation Fraternity**, 621 Plainfield, Suite 308, Willowbrook, Illinois 60521. Phone: (708) 850-7100.

There are two major national associations in the field of trucking. **American Trucking Associations, Inc.** is at 2200 Mill Road, Alexandria, Virginia 22314. **The Professional Truck Driver Institute of America** is a nonprofit group that certifies truck driving training programs, though their standards do not include forfeiture on student loans.

For those who prefer a do-it-yourself approach, the organization offers a *Checklist for Quality Programs in Tractor-Trailer Driving* for four dollars. The address of the **Professional Truck Driver Institute of America** is 8788 Elk Grove Boulevard, Suite M, Elk Grove, California 95624.

For additional advice on truck driving schools, try contacting one of the major trucking firms, such as Werner Enterprises in Omaha. There are several new truck driving programs in community colleges across the country.

Part III

New Learning:
Staying Current in a Changing Economy

Chapter Eighteen

Careers in a New Economy

So the world turns and the workplace churns, as needs and skills and jobs revolve around us. It's a fact of life. For the rest of our careers, you and I will be working in the midst of an economic revolution.

We can't control the pace of a changing economy. But we can try to grasp the shape and direction of change: the shift, for example, from pyramid to diamond-like organizations. Moreover, we can learn to grow with the times. That's the subject of these final two chapters: strategies for guiding our careers in the midst of change, and strategies for lifelong learning.

I believe it's important to have a sense of moving with the times, not only for our professional development but also for our peace of mind. We all need a sense of locomotion. *Business Week* magazine once reported an interesting study of stress in race car drivers. It seems that some researchers at Emory University measured drivers' stress levels when they were traveling at two hundred miles an hour out on the racetrack, then while they were waiting in pit stops as someone else serviced their cars. Conclusion: the drivers experienced far more stress when they gave up control and sat idle.

Another story: A friend of mine met a rabbi in Eastern Europe who had led his congregation through some perilous times during World War II. "We often didn't have enough to eat," said the rabbi. "In fact, we were so short of food, there's no way we'd have survived if we hadn't fasted a lot."

It helps to have a sense of self-control.

As I've already suggested, the best strategy I know for directing the course of our careers these days is to focus on our skills. Skills are our best bridge to the new economy, as well as to the talents that lie within us. Here's a personal example.

A few years ago I decided to take a break from career counseling and try my hand at sports and travel writing. I set out for Canada, where my father had grown up, to write a book on the Canadian Football League. At first I was apprehensive about interviewing football players. I'd never conducted a locker room interview, and wasn't even sure what questions to ask professional athletes. I certainly was no authority on football. My only qualifications were that I'd written a couple of books in other fields.

But after fumbling through a few interviews, I found that I had a valuable transferable skill. As a counselor, I'd spent years listening to people tell me about their lives. And I'd learned how to ask questions in ways that helped them open up and feel comfortable talking. That same skill was just as useful in the locker room or on the practice field. It turned out that interviewing was a bridge between the fields of counseling and journalism.

I've seen the same process repeatedly with mid-career clients. Skills are the bridge from one field to another. Several years ago when I was directing a career counseling program for alumni at the University of Denver, I developed a computer data bank to keep track of my clients according to their work experience and training. One afternoon I was fooling around with the system and began scanning the files of some of the best computer science people in the program. I came up with three who had been especially successful. I printed out their records and spent some time studying them.

As was typical back in the early days of computer professions, none of these individuals had a degree in computer science. One was a lawyer, one a business professional, and the other an ex-priest. But then I noticed a common factor. Each of them had a degree in philosophy from a Jesuit university. Suddenly the light went on. I saw the relevance of rigorous training in critical thinking to both philosophy and computer science.

Then there was the case of Martha, another of my clients who was a geologist. Martha had originally set out to be a landscape artist. Her family had spent vacations at the ocean on the Delaware shore, and Martha loved to paint the seashore. She spent hours watching the changing tides and patterns in the sand. In time she turned out some good watercolors, won a few awards, and took up art in college.

But she changed majors after her sophomore year. It was hard to imagine making a living as an artist. Geology seemed to offer job security. So Martha went on for a degree in geology and then a master's in geophysics.

In Denver in the early 1980s, Martha was making $60,000 a year. The oil companies were into major exploration, and Martha was a gifted geophysicist. She seemed to have a knack for reading seismic charts and sensing where to look for oil reserves. It was almost a sixth sense, like finding patterns in the sand. Then the oil industry collapsed; a hundred thousand jobs were lost in Denver. Martha's employers kept her on as long as they could, hoping they'd resume exploration. But there was little work to fill her time.

Martha looked for ways to keep busy. She began learning more about her computer and got to know a systems analyst in the next department. He introduced her to some fascinating work that was going on in systems analysis. The name of the new field intrigued her. They called it "pattern recognition." It was the same process used in painting, geology, and computer science.

Skills are the bridge from one field to another.

Today there's mounting interest in finding transferable skills in military careers as the nation's defense budget declines. About $1\frac{1}{2}$ million civilian and military defense jobs are slated to be eliminated during the next five years, and the process is already underway.

At Lowry Air Force Base in Denver, one of the installations that's shutting down, personnel officers came up with these observations in publicizing for a job fair, "From Blue Suits to Pinstripes."

"The typical enlisted person almost has an associate's degree completed, has some supervisory experience, and has had anywhere from $25,000 to $100,000 in technical and management training. A typical Air Force captain or major has extensive management experience and probably has one master's degree completed."

Even specialized military skills such as bomb loading may be transferable, as the Air Force sees it: "An Air Force bomb loader could go from managing a supply inventory involving millions of dollars of bombs to overseeing a warehouse full of furniture."

That's an encouraging thought.

Helping military personnel identify and build on their transferable skills is much more effective than simply offering workshops on job search skills, as they've done in the past.

While there's nothing wrong with crafting a good resume (I'm told there are three pages of ads for resume services in the Boston Yellow Pages) or polishing our interviewing techniques, job-search skills are not the stuff of which careers are made. Skills are the basic ingredients. It's how to do a job, not how to get a job, that counts.

The other problem with emphasizing job search strategies is that many books in the field are keyed to the old pyramid-style corporate organizations. They teach techniques, like writing persuasive cover letters or "dressing for success," that are designed to impress someone higher up in some hierarchy—someone who has a job for us. In fact, however, given the reality of today's entrepreneurial, small-business economy, there are few jobs awaiting any of us out there. Instead, most good jobs today are co-created.

Jobs are joint ventures in problem-solving. They're strategies to solve pressing problems in organizations—frequently, more than one problem at a time. For example, consider the cases of two other prospective employers.

✦ ✦ ✦

Sue Langhorn is station manager of KRUD, an all-talk radio station in Slackjaw, Oklahoma. The station converted from Country Western to an all-talk format several years ago when Slackjaw's energy industry was booming. Throngs of business professionals had moved in from the East Coast, and most of them preferred news-radio to Eddie Rabbitt.

But today the station is in trouble. Population has dropped off as the oil boom went bust. Local businesses are struggling. Listener ratings at KRUD are abysmal, and advertising revenue is falling.

Last month, KRUD was sold to a new owner, who inherited a long-term lease in Slackjaw's tallest office building. The lease is a fixed cost from back in the days when business was booming, and the owner finds he can't renegotiate it. The one variable cost the new owner could find was salaries. So last week, he let all his news reporters go. Then he called Sue in and instructed her to come up with other programming ideas. She hasn't slept much since.

Sue knows the all-talk format is a given, since the station has a weak signal. If they were to broadcast music, they couldn't reach the suburbs of Slackjaw. Besides, the majority of advertisers are local firms with an interest in local news coverage. They need all the business information they can get.

The problem is gathering the news with no reporters. Sue sits at her desk and looks down at the floor. Her office is cluttered with local newspapers and business magazines: lots of news, but in the wrong format. What to do? Sue sits in her high-rise office and gazes at the horizon.

✦ ✦ ✦

Ned Benson had never heard of a PRP until he became one. Benson is president of NB Tiling, a building-products company founded by his father. He began working in the business during high school, then set off for college and an MBA. Ned has solid credentials in his industry; he's a good business manager.

But for the past several years he's been spending less time with his business and more time worrying about the local dump. The problem began with a protest by the Sierra Club over some toxic materials found in the bellies of a few dead ducks. A chemist had identified the substance. It was an effluent from NB Tiling. The ducks had eaten it at the dump.

Ned was familiar with the substance, but he'd never known how or where his employees disposed of it. Now the Environmental Protection Agency has identified his company as a "Potentially Responsible Party" for conditions at the dump. As Ned has learned, that's a legal term in Superfund legislation, with fines that can run up to six figures. Anyone who has ever made a deposit in a polluted site can be indicted as a PRP.

Ned has begun to look for help with his new problem. He has a few staff people trained in chemistry, and a corporate attorney. But no one seems equipped to work at the boundaries of business management, environmental science, and law. Last week some forms arrived from the EPA, with an announcement of a hearing next month. Is there anyone to help a PRP?

The solutions to problems such as Sue's and Ned's often must be co-created. They're multiple problems that call for more than one perspective. That's why many employers use the interview process to explore fresh approaches to their problems with prospective employees. For example, if Sue were to interview local English teachers or newspaper reporters, she might come up with a job for someone who could rewrite articles in print so they could be read on the air, using short words and simple sentences. Were she to find a writer with a good speaking voice, that person might double as an announcer.

Ned might begin looking for lawyers trained in the sciences, or a biologist with an MBA—both by advertising a job description and scouring universities that offer degree programs in environmental management or health. He also might sign up for a course in hazardous substance management such as those sponsored by the National Environmental Health Association.

While both situations may sound daunting, they're also typical of the way jobs in this changing economy are created every day. *The best new jobs are multi-problem positions that call for innovative solutions and unconventional combinations of skills.* Like the cases of Jeff and Laurel cited in chapter 3, the stories of Sue and Ned are based on fact. There are many new hybrid jobs like Sue's in the changing world of media, and Ned's case is typical of firms that are hiring graduates of new academic programs in environmental management and health. That's why the abilities to think creatively and stay in touch with our skills are much more important than spending time polishing our resumes or honing our interviewing techniques. Skills are the stuff from which we can co-create a position for ourselves with a prospective employer.

Just as jobs are joint ventures, *employers are partners* in the problem-solving process. Much as we're accustomed to thinking of a prospective employer as a parent figure who's prone to hire the candidate with the best-shined shoes, nowadays that's mostly not the case. Employers are more like partners in a joint venture. Employers may be younger than the people they hire, for one thing. Almost every mentor I've had in the field of journalism has been at least fifteen years my junior. Today's fluid economy is like that; it's a place where jobs are created as people trade skills in small, diamond-like organizations. Jobs are joint ventures; employers are partners.

Which leads to my third point. *A career is a continuing education.* The bottom-line benefit in most jobs is what we learn, not what we earn. As an instructor in aviation mechanics told me the other day, "Our field is changing so fast that a diploma is nothing but a license to keep on learning." That's why a good short-term strategy in seeking employment is to look for a good learning environment in an industry where one wants to be—even if the first available job isn't one where you want to stay. The point is to hire on and learn the ropes in a good learning community.

For the long term, I believe in focusing on the kinds of issues or problems one cares about and building skills to address those concerns. For example, I find it helpful to address problems of employment as a writer, teacher, and researcher. It's good to have more than one tool in one's toolbox.

Imagine these three circles as a set of skills, with an industry, a job role, a region of the world, or perhaps a certain social concern as the focal point.

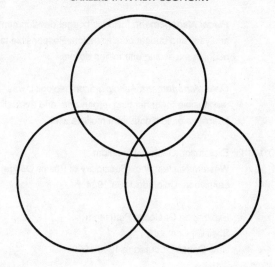

If you're interested in concurrent engineering, for example, the three rings would represent skills in product design, manufacturing, and marketing. In the field of alternative dispute resolution, your set of skills might include arbitration, mediation, and negotiation. Whatever your field of interest, don't think specialization; think in threes.

Here is a good resume format for summarizing our skills. This individual is one of the geologists described in chapter 3, who was trying to connect his skills with other fields such as environmental management. Notice how his transferable skills are summarized under Capabilities. It's a way of helping people in other fields understand what a geologist can do.

FRED

Address

Phone

SUMMARY OF QUALIFICATIONS:	Project manager with extensive experience in energy industry, and special interest in data management.
CAPABILITIES:	***Project Management:*** Experienced in full range of management functions including defining program objectives, budgeting, supervision of personnel, coordination of contractors, analyzing data, and communicating recommendations. Experienced in coordination with government agencies.

Fiscal Management: Includes budget development, cost analysis, and budget administration. Responsible for annual budgets exceeding one million dollars.

Data Management: As exploration geologist, was responsible for generating, organizing, and evaluating large quantities of field data from multiple sites.

EMPLOYMENT: Exploration Geologist-Uranium
Western Nuclear, Inc. (Subsidiary of Phelps Dodge)
Lakewood, Colorado 1969-1984

Exploration Geologist-Petroleum
Shell Oil Company
New Orleans, Louisiana 1966-1969

EDUCATION: MS-Geology 1966
University of Wyoming

BS-Geology 1963
Florida State University

NEW LEARNING: Sailing, photography, antique clock collecting, home computing.

Sometimes the mix of skills we learn is dictated by the labor market. That was true of Marsha and Larry McVey (described in chapter 14), who found themselves managing apartments as a result of a bad real estate investment. Their expertise in residential management was essentially a strategy for economic survival.

Other times, the skills people develop seem driven by their values. Sarah Edwards, one of the nation's leading authorities on home-based businesses, entered that field and completely revamped her skills because of a powerful personal experience. In the late 1960s, Sarah was a social worker employed by the federal government in Kansas City, Missouri. She served as a regional consultant to Head Start programs and was constantly on the go, flying to meet clients all over the Midwest. At the same time, she was occupied with maintaining a home for herself and her husband Paul and their two-year-old son.

It was a stimulating lifestyle, till one day she collapsed. "I'd thought I was doing fine," she remembers, "but my body didn't agree."

Sarah was hospitalized with a kidney infection, so run-down that she almost died. When the doctor came to see her, he said, "We almost lost you last night. I want you to know that your illness is life-style-related. You are doing yourself in."

That conversation caught her attention, but didn't provide a solution to her problem. "Here I had a career and a husband and a child, and I didn't have any idea how I was going to juggle all of this," she says.

One night she had a meeting with another consultant at his office, which turned out to be in his home. "He seemed to have an incredibly comfortable life," she recalls. "Here we were meeting in his conference room, along with his dog."

Sarah began to consider how she might work out of her own home. Eventually she went back to school to become licensed as a clinical social worker, then opened a psychotherapy practice in a home-based office. Before long, Paul joined her. An attorney who ran a research and consulting firm in downtown Kansas City, he relocated his business to another room in their home.

Today the Edwards are full-time consultants to other home-based, "open-collar" workers across the nation. Authors of four books, they also write a magazine column, host a network radio program, and manage a Working From Home forum for twenty-five thousand subscribers on CompuServe. That's in addition to conducting a constant round of lectures and seminars.

The Edwards now live in Santa Monica, California, on the outskirts of Los Angeles, where many of their neighbors commute two hours each way to and from work. They're constantly reminded of the need for new options such as home-based businesses.

"We see families getting up at 5:00 in the morning, packing their kids up and schlepping them over to day care while they're still sleeping," Sarah says. "They're carrying them over their shoulder, putting them in day care, driving to work, coming home, then picking them up again. In other words, they leave their kids off in the dark and they pick their kids up in the dark."

It was six years after the Edwards opened their own home offices that the idea of becoming consultants to other home-based businesses took hold.

In 1980, Sarah attended a conference to commemorate the 100th anniversary of the birth of Teilhard de Chardin, the Catholic philospher of evolution. It was a "hands-on" conference, with the workshops to help participants evaluate their own evolution: their sense of mission and purpose on earth. For Sarah, the conference was a pivotal experience.

"While I was there," she says, "I had a vision—one of those things where your mind pops. I saw the changes that were going to be happening in our society, and that the transition was going to be very painful for a lot of people, and I saw the contribution that we could make to help people make that transition.

As Sarah looks at the future course of her own career, the vision of helping people run businesses from their homes still occupies center stage. "There are all kinds of issues yet to be addressed, such as legal problems and legislation," she says. "Those will require other skills. But I'm sure this will be my work for the rest of my life."

Paul adds, "When she came back and told me her idea, then I got excited. Up till then, we'd each had our own businesses, but this was something we could do together."

That's what happens when we find clarity in our careers. It helps us make contact with others. If we're in touch with our own work-related values, then we're likely to find ourselves in a position to network with other people who share our interests and concerns.

Networking can be a deliberate, strategic process as we search out a place where someone wants what we can do. When exploring a new field, I recommend the following strategy. First, orient yourself to the industries and job roles of the field. Ask dumb questions of someone who's not a prospective employer. Then look into the needs of particular organizations where you might be interested in working. Finally, zero in on specific employers to get a clear idea of what they need before you approach anyone for a job. The idea is to find a match between their needs and your skills. As the late career writer John Crystal put it, the prime question is, "What needs doing?" (see chart facing page).

I've used this method in my own career when approaching fields where I had no experience, such as journalism. At other times, I've found the process of networking happens almost naturally. Back in the early 1970s, I was struggling with my work as a college chaplain in suburban Chicago. It was a role I'd enjoyed ten years before, but now I was in my mid-thirties and getting a bit old to chum around with undergraduates. I knew I was trouble when I couldn't get excited about the Beatles.

It seemed the only part of my job I enjoyed was setting up internships for students in social service agencies around the city. That's how I'd come to know one of the leaders in a large voluntary service agency, and she'd asked me to take part in a radio talk show.

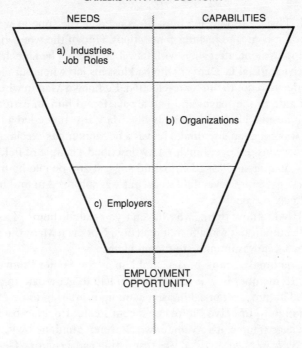

It was one of those dry panel discussions broadcast for insomniacs in the dead of night.

So one night at 2:00 a.m. I found myself in a studio of WBBM in downtown Chicago, fighting to stay awake. I struck up a conversation with the fellow sitting next to me during a commercial break. It turned out he'd been lining up internships for students at a new program called University Without Walls. His interests were similar to mine.

"So how's the program going?" I mumbled, stifling a yawn.

"Not bad, except we can't seem to find a director," he replied. "It's a three-year, grant-funded position. Know anyone who'd be interested?"

I came to life.

Within a month I was working in that job and launched into a new career in adult education. Years later, looking back on the encounter, I know it was no fluke. I met the man who was trying to fill that position because we already inhabited an invisible network of people who shared the same approach to education. All that had remained was to meet.

Schools, professional associations, and other learning organizations are wonderful places to network—especially if we're unemployed. That's a time when most of us need all the support we can get when it comes to making connections. One of the worst effects of unemployment, after all, is withdrawal. Recently I had lunch with an ex-civic official in Denver who had lost his job when our former mayor decided not to run for re-election. I'd known Marvin when he was an aide to the mayor and had always found him an extremely helpful person. There was nobody like Marv, if you needed a bit of information or even a referral. He was a networker par excellence.

As we visited over lunch, Marv described a couple of fields he was researching and asked if I could suggest any people he might contact. I gave him several referrals, but was surprised to find he already knew the people.

"If you know them, why haven't you called them?" I asked him. He admitted it was a fear of rejection. Not even Marv, the master-networker, was immune to the problem.

Sometimes I think of that problem as the Senior Prom Syndrome. Remember how it felt when you had to get a date to a big dance? The prospect of calling someone up or waiting to be called was enough to unnerve Norman Vincent Peale. Looking back on that teenage trauma, it's a wonder we all weren't undone by it.

The reason we survived was that dating had a context. Getting dates was only one strand in the larger fabric of high-school life. We made contact with the opposite sex and got clues as to who might be available as we mingled in the halls each day at school. High school provided a support system for traumatic events such as finding a date to the prom. It was an antidote to the anxieties of adolescence.

As an adult, I find our needs are not so different. We still need some systems of support and points of connection with others. The difference is that, as we grow up, those contacts are harder to come by. In adulthood we're much more isolated.

That's one of the strongest arguments I know for pursuing some course of study when we're unemployed: not just to learn new skills, but also to make contact with others whose interests are leading them in a similar direction. Learning is the leading edge of our experience, and education is a source of community.

The basic questions in every career are:

+ What needs doing?
+ What can you do? and
+ What have you been learning?

Chapter Nineteen

Lifelong Learning

As anyone who's been a parent can attest, learning is as natural as breathing. Watch an infant develop. See the incredible range of competencies of a two-year-old, and it's impossible to doubt that human beings have a strong interest in acquiring new skills. It's a need that doesn't diminish with age. Adults enjoy learning just as much as kids do.

But adult learning is complicated; as grown-ups we have other roles and responsibilities in our lives. Beyond that, there are tough choices involved in continuing one's education. What if the skills we learn should land us in a dead-end job? Or in no job at all?

We've all heard stories of professionals who quit their jobs to earn an advanced degree, then ended up as parking-lot cashiers after graduation. It's tough to be a good consumer of education.

Today there are many colleges with special degree programs for working adults. Add to that the many other learning options outside schools, and it's no wonder that adult learners face some pretty perplexing choices. In this closing chapter, I'll highlight some of the typical questions most of us face when we consider continuing our education. Two issues are often especially important to adult learners. One is finding our academic comfort zone, and the other is resolving the riddle of academic credentials.

As an introduction, since we're looking at learning, let's start with a quiz. Pencils ready? Here we go.

What do these world-famous authors have in common: Stephen Crane, Eugene O'Neill, William Faulkner, F. Scott Fitzgerald? Answer: all of them flunked out of college.

Some notable figures have, in fact, done worse than that. Emile Zola, the French novelist, once got a score of zero on his literature exams. As you've guessed, the moral of the quiz is that many

productive people have succeeded not because of—but in spite of—
their experiences in school.

Cradles of Eminence, a 1960s best seller that analyzed the childhood experiences of several hundred international celebrities, found
that 60 percent had hated school. "It is, in fact, nothing short of a
miracle that the modern methods of instruction have not yet entirely
strangled the holy curiosity of inquiry," wrote one of the subjects.
That was Albert Einstein.

I understand his feelings. Although I've taught college courses
for years, I still find that my ego shrivels whenever I assume the role
of classroom student. It's the result of some bad experiences I had in
junior and senior high school.

A few years ago I took a Spanish course with a vibrant Mexican
woman I liked very much. But every time she called on me in class,
I became tongue-tied. I couldn't remember Spanish words I'd
known when I enrolled in the class.

The last night of class, we all went out to a Mexican restaurant.
Our teacher, as usual, spoke only in Spanish. Halfway through the
evening, I realized that I was replying in Spanish as well.

The teacher looked at me quizzically. "*Su Espanol es mejor con
dos cervezas*," she noted. She was right. Two beers, and my Spanish
got a whole lot better.

Over the years, I've met many adults who are stalled in their
careers because of education-related anxieties. Some have attended
three or four colleges without ever having completed a degree.
Some are unable to do simple math. Some can scarcely read.

I remember one woman I taught in a course for adults who
were returning to college. She was a bright woman who felt stuck in
a secretarial position. Moving up required a college degree, but
she'd never been able to complete one. Several years later, I happened to run into her again, and was surprised to find she'd become
director of training at a large financial association. It turned out that
she'd gone on to graduate from the college where we'd met.

She told me, "That course you taught changed my life."

"What's that?" I asked. (No one had ever accused me of being
that good a lecturer.) "What was it about the course that was so
meaningful?"

"It was the test you gave us," she said. "When I took that test
and we discussed it, I realized for the first time that I have special
needs as a learner. That test taught me to look for schools and
classes where I can meet my needs."

The test was an instrument I've used for years, known as the

Learning Style Inventory. It was devised by David Kolb, a social psychologist who became interested in learning styles when he served as an academic advisor at the Massachusetts Institute of Technology. (I've also mentioned his work earlier in the book.)

Kolb noticed that many bright students dropped out of MIT—not because they couldn't do the work required but because they learned in a different manner from the engineers who ran the school. He went on to study the various ways in which specialists in different fields pursue learning. Some interesting differences turned up. He found that engineers, for example, tend to follow a very concrete learning style; they like questions that can be answered right-or-wrong. Social workers, on the other hand, do better with creative material such as case studies.

Kolb's research suggests that all of us should pay attention to our comfort zones in learning. Be it small seminars or large lecture classes, independent study or on-the-job training, we should each find the mode that fits us best. Some of us will do better in active styles, while others need time for quiet reflection. Wherever possible, we ought to negotiate for a style of learning that matches our strengths. That's part of being a good educational consumer. We should ask questions of schools and instructors, make our needs known, and ask ourselves some hard questions. "How will this course be taught?" "Does that match the way I learn best?"

The student who finally finished her degree was a person who didn't learn well in a traditional classroom with rows of chairs and a professor lecturing at the blackboard. But put her in an active learning role, such as an internship, and she blossomed. Fortunately, the school where we met offered many such opportunities.

Sometimes, of course, our needs can't be met in a class we must take. If we find ourselves consigned to an uncomfortable setting—a classroom or teacher that just doesn't fit—it's important to recognize that's not our style, and not to criticize ourselves for having trouble. Sometimes the subject matter is in a field where we'll always have trouble.

For me, that's technical material. If I have to learn how to operate a computer software program or assemble a lawn chair, I know that I must be kind to myself. I need to take plenty of time with frequent breaks, and find someone to whom I can read parts of the technical instructions aloud.

The point is to get past the notion that education must be a one-size-fits-all experience, and to negotiate for the kinds of learning settings where we're likely to succeed. That's partly a matter of recognizing and honoring our personal learning style.

Kolb seems to view learning as a form of problem-solving. We learn in order to get past some impediment in our lives—whether it's setting up a computer or just crawling across the living room to pull down a lamp. He believes there are four phases in a typical problem-solving/learning cycle. First, we *perceive* the problem to be solved, then we *process* what we've seen and heard to form a concept or theory of it. After that, we *produce* some sort of solution to the problem; and, finally, we *promote* our solution to the problem to others. (The four terms are my translations of his more academic terminology.)

Just as we each have preferences in the four phases of the problem-solving cycle, so our skills also follow different patterns. We each tend to develop skills that follow our most comfortable style of learning. As a result, we develop distinctive weaknesses and strengths. Employers must address those differences whenever they fill a job. Imagine a president-elect of the United States considering candidates for a Cabinet position. One candidate may have strong *perceptions* of the problems to be addressed by his department. Frequently such people are described as having "lived" the problems (such as Henry Cisneros, President Clinton's Secretary of Housing and Urban Development, who grew up in poverty). Another person may be highly analytical—perhaps a college professor who has *processed* theoretical solutions to certain problems—such as Secretary of Labor Robert Reich. A third candidate may be a hands-on problem-solver who enjoys technical tasks such as writing legislation. That's the way Jimmy Carter is said to have conducted his presidency. Finally, there's the promoting kind of person who may be fuzzy on the details of his job but has the ability to put his point across—such as President Ronald Reagan, the Great Communicator.

Ideally, a presidential cabinet will include people from all these types, as will each department. After all, just as all four phases of the problem-solving cycle are vitally important, it's equally true that none of us has equal ability in all areas. That's why as individuals we need to recognize our strengths and get help in the areas where we're less comfortable: both in our work and in our learning.

Here's an exercise I sometimes use to help people consider the four phases of problem-solving in relation to themselves.

PERSONAL SKILLS PROFILE

Directions:
1. Read through the lists of skills below. Check the words that represent something you can do.
2. Place a second check beside each word that represents something you do well.
3. Circle those skills you especially enjoy using.

Promoting Skills

administering	inspiring
advocating	leading
addressing	managing
assigning	marketing
bargaining	motivating
coordinating	negotiating
delegating	organizing
enlisting	persuading
evaluating	publicizing
expediting	selling
facilitating	supervising
initiating	team-building

Perceiving Skills

asking	identifying
assisting	interpreting
caring	listening
collaborating	perceiving
communicating	recommending
contributing	reconciling
counseling	resolving
consulting	responding
encouraging	sensing
entertaining	serving
explaining	supporting
helping	understanding

Producing Skills

assembling	operating
building	programming
cataloging	recording
compiling	renovating
computing	repairing
constructing	reproducing
designing	scanning
drawing	shaping
gathering	tabulating
grouping	troubleshooting
maintaining	updating
making	visualizing

Processing Skills

assessing	outlining
clarifying	reading
classifying	reasoning
defining	reporting
detailing	researching
detecting	reviewing
diagnosing	solving
editing	studying
examining	summarizing
investigating	systematizing
judging	thinking
memorizing	verifying

Look over the columns you have marked. Which are darker than the others? The kinds of skills each of us develops from an important personal path in worklife.

Kolb's Learning Style Inventory and a related instrument, the Personal Learning Guide, suggest strategies for choosing learning settings that play to individual strengths. Processing types, for example, often do well in independent study where they can spend a lot of time alone with their thoughts. Promoting types often thrive on interaction.

Today there's a great variety of degree programs for working adults: the "new traditional students." Some of them offer distinctive options for mid-life learners. Bob Gambles, age twenty-eight, found his niche at the University of Phoenix. Gambles was only thirty credits short of a degree at Arizona State University when he decided to drop out of school.

Part of his problem was time. Gambles was employed as a television producer for a public broadcasting station while he was taking classes. It was a stimulating job with lots of learning potential. But none of his courses at ASU related to his learning on the job. He says Arizona State dealt with students en masse, regardless of their experience.

"After a while it was difficult to get excited about participating in 'discussion groups' with seventy other students," he recalls.

Today Gambles is back in school at the University of Phoenix, an academic institution designed to build on the experience of working adults. University of Phoenix students average thirty-five years of age. They must be employed as a condition of admittance. Classes are held in the evening, once a week. Other assignments are completed independently and in small study groups, to which students belong throughout their academic program.

The basic curriculum at the U. of Phoenix consists of eighteen courses running five weeks each. While subjects and instructors change, the students remain in the same, four-member study groups. If there's a problem sharing the work load, the students must resolve it. They all receive the same grade for their projects.

Case material for the courses often comes from the experience of study group members. Gambles' group completed a feasibility study for a fellow-student's business venture. They became immersed in the trials of America West Airlines through a group member who worked there. The airline had set out to achieve $2 billion in sales at any cost, and did—at a cost of $2.3 billion. It was a case study in the hazards of promotional campaigns and fare discounts.

To graduate from the University of Phoenix, each student must complete a work-related project to demonstrate individual competence. But the basic exercise is learning to work effectively in small groups. It's a collaborative rather than competitive approach to

education. For Gambles, the study group experience has made a
world of difference. He says, "It's the process of the program that I
enjoy most. It's applicable to any field."

Just as individuals differ in learning styles, so do professional
groups. Professions tend to cultivate the same core competencies, so
when a profession changes, co-workers often have common learning
needs. I often help members of professional associations take stock
of the ways their work is changing, and consider how they can learn
effectively together. One of the most interesting groups I've met
with recently is an association of financial planners. The profession
is scarcely thirty years old, but already it's changing radically.

Ten or twelve years ago, when personal computers and spreadsheet software entered the field of financial planning, the planners
and their clients became enamored of long-range investment
schemes. Planners would gather all kinds of data from their clients,
pour it all into their computers, and spin out lifetime plans. That's
when processing skills were in vogue. But during the past five or six
years, many of those long-range plans have gone up in smoke.
That's because the economy has become so uncertain that cradle-to-
grave financial schemes don't hold up as they once did. More people
are in a survival mode, living month-to-month—just trying to get by.

The other new factor is that more Americans are living longer.
As financial planners deal with aging clients, they find themselves
asked to provide assistance with tasks of daily living, such as buying
a car. As a result, many financial planners find they're functioning
more as social workers than analytical specialists. They need to develop more sensitive perceiving skills. That's typical of the way in
which members of a profession may find themselves shifting gears
all at the same time—from the core competencies in which they
were originally trained to new needs for cross-training. That's why
some of the most dynamic learning today is occurring in professional
associations. Some of the most enjoyable learning, too. The best associations meld learning with play, as children do.

I sat in on a recent meeting of the Data Processing Management Association in Denver on a frigid evening in mid-February. A
roomful of computer scientists was decked out in flowered shirts and
leis. It was Hawaiian Luau Night. Throughout the program, between
technical talks, the president of DPMA raffled off macadamia nuts.

The main speaker was an international authority on global
telecommunication networks: a heady subject. But as soon as the
applause died down after his talk, the scientist found himself drawing numbers for macadamia nuts.

I observed a couple of before-dinner workshops on management issues. One session dealt with alcohol abuse in the workplace. It was only semi-serious. ("Every time I'd go hunting," a recovering alcoholic recalled, "I'd get drunk and shoot my truck. But I learned my lesson. After a while, I didn't take my truck.")

The following workshop on project management ended abruptly after half an hour when the leader glanced at her watch and proposed, "Let's knock off and get a drink." She obviously had nothing against a little well-timed alcohol abuse.

I was impressed by the tone of the proceedings. Here were some of the best-trained computer professionals in Colorado, yet they never seemed to take themselves or one another very seriously. At the same time, as with most good associations, the mission of DPMA was plenty serious. The group sponsors scholarships for students entering the field. One graduate student who was taking a course in ethics distributed a questionnaire on ethical issues in networked computers (Who should have access to salary schedules and personnel records?).

DPMA belongs to a larger organization, the Institute for Certification of Computer Professionals, that sponsors a series of forbidding exams in computer technology. It's the kind of professional evaluation system that was once the province of universities. To date, over forty-two thousand computer professionals have been tested by the ICCP.

Another group with a serious agenda is the Public Relations Society of America. Public relations has traveled a rocky road in recent years. The problem, as with other white-collar professions, is a loss of corporate jobs. Wes Poriotis, a Madison Avenue executive recruiter who specializes in public relations, estimates that 20 percent of all professionals in the field are "traumatized, hard-core unemployed."

Paradoxically, many of the p.r. people who have lost their jobs are some of the most highly-trained specialists in their profession. But that's part of their problem. Like other corporate specialists, their skills are too refined for today's rough-and-tumble small-business market.

Small businesses need public relations consultants; they just can't afford full-time staff people. And the skills they need from consultants cover the entire range of the field—everything from publications to media relations to managing special events. Small-business owners need p.r. generalists.

That's where the corporate specialists are in trouble. While they may have taken a range of public relations courses in school, the subjects have changed in recent years. A corporate specialist who has concentrated on staging special events, for example, is unlikely to have spent much time learning desktop publishing software for turning out newsletters.

To become marketable once again, many public relations professionals need to be retrained as generalists. That's what the Denver chapter of the Public Relations Society of America began to realize several years ago. Leaders of the group had been stung by an editorial Poriotis had published as a paid advertisement in a p.r. trade journal. He'd addressed it to the PRSA and another national professional group, the International Association of Business Communicators.

"If I were to bring a class action suit against the officers of your two associations," Poriotis began, "it would be on behalf of the 'walking wounded' unemployed among your respective memberships whose pain and suffering go ignored while your organizations go about their business as if all is normal . . . . Many have not worked in the last two or three years. Yet, they continue to keep up appearances and claim to be consultants or free-lance workers . . . .

"Your real job now is to bring resources and survival kits to the victims of public relations genocide . . . . Create projects and special teams to help the unemployed repackage themselves. Charge fees to the employed to hear your programs on how to avoid the pink slip in their respective companies. And, like the trade unions did during the first depression, set aside a portion of such fees and your own financial resources in a fund. If out-of-work steel workers can dip into a union fund, why should your hungry, your needy, and your deserving professionals have any less?"

Poriotis' editorial is an especially graphic description of the dilemma many white-collar professional groups face today. On the one hand, they're organizations of independent professionals who aren't accustomed to giving or receiving hand-outs. White-collar workers want to stand on their own two feet. On the other hand, many members of these professions are hurting badly, and they're unlikely to keep paying membership dues. Organizations that fail to respond to survival issues such as unemployment are themselves unlikely to survive long in a recession.

The editorial found its mark in Denver. Numerous public relations jobs had been lost in the late-1980s energy industry downturn, leaving corporate specialists walking the streets. PRSA decided that education was one way to address the problem. A few years before, the local chapter had instituted a mentoring program for recent college grads who were entering the field. Suppose the program were expanded to include mid-career people? It was a reasonable idea. Then someone else had another idea. What if those who served as mentors could receive mentoring as well? That might be a way to strengthen relationships within the organization, in the course of expanding skills.

That's what the group has done. Today, thirty-eight members of the Denver chapter serve as mentors, of whom eleven have mentors themselves. It's a loosely organized program with a few published guidelines ("meals and drinks are Dutch treat") and lots of room for innovation. Each year, prospective mentors and "mentees" check off their areas of expertise and learning interests on a special form: Advertising, Consumer Affairs, Media Relations, etc. There are seventeen categories in all. Then a program coordinator makes introductions, and the mentors and mentees are off and running.

I interviewed a couple of the pairs and found some interesting stories. A displaced corporate specialist in technical writing was paired with an experienced small-business consultant. One of his first concerns was learning procedures for billing: "Do you charge for travel time?"

Another ex-corporate employee found himself working for a downtown development organization. It was a totally different brand of public relations from his former job with a military contractor. "Out there we were always in a defensive mode, trying to keep the press at bay," he told me. "Here, the idea is to initiate activity."

The Denver mentoring program illustrates some of the possible roles professional associations might play in today's changing economy. While they may not fill every niche of traditional organized labor, there are many needs they can meet by being in close communication with their members. One of the first and best challenges is retraining.

A matter of degrees

All of which raises the question of academic credentials. In a society where there's so much informal learning in professional associations, franchising organizations, small-business organizations, and even temporary-employment services, do college and graduate degrees matter anymore? The question is especially pertinent to cities like Denver, where there are more highly credentialed white-collar workers than white-collar jobs. At last count, for example, 60 percent of the meter readers at the public utilities company held college degrees.

Meanwhile, colleges continue to shake the bushes for students with all sorts of come-ons, as in this brochure from the University of Colorado at Denver: "With a highly prized University of Colorado degree, most students find they easily meet an employer's specific needs and their own career objectives." Tell that to a meter reader with a college degree.

Just how valuable is a college degree these days? Is it worth going back to school to get one? Here are some facts to consider.

On the one hand, it's important to note that more and more Americans have college degrees. In 1970 there were 11.8 million college grads in the United States. By 1990, that number had increased almost three-fold to 32.5 million. The fastest-growing group of students was women aged thirty-five and older, whose numbers quadrupled between 1970 and 1990. Currently, 90 percent of employers in the U.S. offer tuition reimbursement as part of their employee benefit plans; 97 percent are expected to offer the benefit by the year 2000 (source: *Lifelong Learning Trends*, published by the National University Continuing Education Association in Washington, D.C.).

Credit for prior learning

In recent years, colleges and universities have taken steps to recognize the skills that mature students bring to the classroom. Many mid-career adults now find they can receive academic credit for non-classroom learning through procedures known as "prior learning assessment." They can cut the time required to earn a degree and avoid sitting through classes they might be qualified to teach.

According to the National University Continuing Education Association, 97 percent of America's higher education institutions now grant credit for prior learning. But the methods they use differ, as do the amounts of credit they assign. Here are three common approaches to the assessment of prior learning.

Testing. Today, 93 percent of the nation's colleges and universities award credit based on exams. The tests are of two kinds. Some are standard tests, such as the College Board's College Level Examination Program. CLEP exams test knowledge from courses that are similar from one college to the next, such as introductory biology or calculus. DANTES (the Defense Activity for Non-Traditional Education Support) is a similar set of exams for military personnel. The credits are transferable. Pass a standard test in a common subject, and you can apply that credit to a broad range of schools.

Some schools also offer "challenge" exams for their own

courses. Pass the test and you'll receive credit for the course—but only from that institution. You can't transfer the credit to another school, as you could with a CLEP exam.

Published Guides. The American Council on Education evaluates training programs of some 230 large corporations and government agencies, to determine whether they're equivalent to certain college courses. You might have completed a course, say, in a computer software program that may qualify for credit from a college that teaches the same subject. Some 40 percent of American colleges provide this kind of prior learning credit.

Portfolio Assessment. About 33 percent of U.S. colleges offer students the opportunity to identify learning that may pertain to their degree, if they can supply evidence of their knowledge. For example, a student in human services may have learned to use sign language in a social service agency. If the director of that agency certified the learning, the college would grant credit. As with the published guide approach, portfolio credit from one school is not transferable to others.

Those are two arguments for completing a college degree: more of our competitors in the workplace have one, and there's the possibility of earning credit for what one has learned in the school of hard knocks.

Another, related, argument is that college grads seem to be doing much better than non-grads. According to figures compiled by the Center for Labor Market Studies at Northeastern University in Boston, the income gap between male college graduates and high-school grads more than doubled between 1973 and 1986. Paul Harrington, a labor economist at Northeastern, is quick to point out that colleges may not be entirely responsible for the relative success of their graduates. "The main reason the rate of return is so good for college grads," he observes, "is that the labor market treats everyone else so bad."

Harrington believes that non-college graduates have suffered from the loss of "bridge jobs" in manufacturing—the kinds of jobs where people could learn basic skills and work their way up the ladder of pyramid organizations. He points out that today, only half as many young adults are working in manufacturing as thirty years ago.

Look at the jobs in diamond organizations and it's easy to see why more people are returning to college. The points of entry in those firms are not at the bottom of some work-your-way-up ladder, but in the middle of the organizations—where new workers must be able to hit the deck running, with marketable skills in place.

So it's possible to argue that anyone who can possibly earn a college sheepskin ought to. That's not to mention all the non-economic values of higher education for life-enrichment.

The questions begin to surface when one considers the relationship between where today's college graduates are employed on the one hand and their major fields of study on the other. With the exception of a few occupations in the health sciences, it seems that college grads with the same degrees are scattered all over the map. To cite just a few examples, according to the economists at Northeastern, only one journalism grad in four is employed in publishing five years after graduation, and only 17 percent of banking and finance grads are working in commercial banks. In the field of information sciences and computer systems, graduates are so scattered that no one industry employs even 10 percent of them. The office-machine industry is the largest employer, with 9.7 percent.

Today it seems the basic purpose of a college education is to generate long-term generalists. That is, if one can leave college with enough skills to gain a foothold in some occupation—learning to do research as a journalist, for example—then it may be possible to expand upon those skills as one shifts to other fields. A good education is one that enables a person to recycle skills repeatedly.

And I do mean "repeatedly." For, in most fields, higher education has become a lifelong process—whether or not one has a degree. It's no longer the four-years-in-and-out gambit it used to be. A college education is not so much a possession as a process.

That's especially evident in community colleges. One of the most ambiguous institutions in America, the community college was founded by President Harry Truman after World War II. The idea was to establish a place where high-school grads who weren't ready for a full, four-year university could study for a couple of years until they were ready to do so.

Today there are some 1,200 community colleges across the country—enrollment has been growing twice as fast as in four-year colleges—and their mission is much more diverse. The typical community college student today is thirty years of age (in many schools, 20 percent of entering students already have undergraduate degrees), and the skills taught run the gamut. As Neale Baxter of the *Occupational Outlook Quarterly* puts it, ". . . no two schools are alike. With so many community colleges, each trying to tailor its programs to the needs of the local area, the only standard is variety."

Michigan's schools feature programs in manufacturing technology—a major emphasis in economic development efforts throughout that state—while Santa Fe Community College in Florida offers a degree in zoo animal technology. Meanwhile, a recent list of award-winning programs nationwide includes everything from aviation maintenance and fluid-power technology to training programs in law enforcement and supermarket occupations.

The main emphasis at most community colleges is providing technical training for occupations that require not four years' but two years' worth of skills. That includes many of today's most promising jobs. In the field of environmental technology, for example, a recent survey of environmental officials showed that 62 percent of the managers expect that 81 percent of the workers they hire for environmental remediation will be technicians with Associate of Arts degrees. In contrast, only 10 percent of new employees will require four-year college degrees. (The study was conducted by the National Center for Research in Vocational Education at the University of California at Berkeley.)

Don Goodwin calls the workers in these new two-year-training jobs "technoprofessionals." He believes they're vitally important to America's new economy. Goodwin serves as president of the Texas State Technical College at Waco—part of a statewide, four-campus program in advanced technical education. Originally trained as a vocational-arts teacher, he has taken on the fascinating challenge of converting a former U.S. Air Force Base to a two-year college. (I mentioned his work in an earlier chapter.)

The college offers a dozen high-tech courses of study in everything from environmental studies to aeronautics. Computer-supported manufacturing is a major field, with nine million dollars' worth of new equipment. There's another forty million dollars' worth of laser technology on campus. The mission of the school is to produce graduates for a new class of jobs in advanced technology.

"We've always viewed manufacturing work environments as hot and dirty sweatshops," Goodwin says. "But the reality is that most workplaces for today's technicians are hygienically pure and environmentally controlled. Plus, they pay well."

They certainly do, if one can judge by the salaries of Goodwin's graduates. In 1991, the placement rate for TSTC-Waco grads was 86 percent. In high-tech programs it was 100 percent. The average starting salary was $28,000 a year. Two graduates from a specialized two-year curriculum started at $72,000 each.

The curriculum, of course, is not what one thinks of as "technical/vocational education," such as auto mechanics and industrial arts. It's chock full of advanced math and science courses such as college algebra, calculus, and chemistry. That's because the new tech-noprofessional jobs are just that; they call for skilled, "tech-know-professional" workers.

Today, in one field after another, some of the best-paying and most satisfying jobs involve skills drawn from the traditionally separate realms of manual and intellectual occupations. Neither blue-collar nor white-collar, they're jobs for new generalists. In this book we've seen many examples of technoprofessionals. They include registered nurses, some of whom make $50,000 a year; dental hygienists earning over $30,000; and automotive technicians who may earn anywhere from $50,000 to $100,000 annually. Compare the earning potential and job security of these skilled technicians to traditional white-collar professionals such as lawyers and architects, and it's evident there's no comparison. The outlook for technoprofessionals is much more favorable.

One reason for the shift to technical generalist jobs is the influence of advanced technology in all sorts of industries. Automotive technicians are paid to service on-board computers that have doubled the gas mileage cars got twenty years ago while drastically reducing pollution. There are more of these computers in many cars than on the earliest flights into space, which is why automotive maintenance has become such a high-tech occupation.

That's one reason we're seeing more generalists in the American workplace: because technology is changing. Another reason is the change I've noted in organizations, from corporate pyramids to diamond-shaped organizations. In today's flatter, more flexible firms, workers must perform a wide range of functions, independently.

I once tried to explain America's community colleges to a visiting German labor official. I told him that the schools offered short-term training in technical skills, at low tuition. That's why so many older Americans enroll. I rattled off the statistics. Average student aged thirty, many entering students already holding four-year college degrees.

With a structured, European mind-set, he struggled to understand what I was saying. "If you already have a degree and I'm just starting college, how in the world can I compete with you?" he asked. I suggested that competition was not the point. Community colleges are an open learning environment where all sorts of people can go to update their skills.

Afterward, I thought that telling him this story might have helped. I was touring a community college when I ran into a retired printer who was taking courses in graphic design. I asked him how he liked the classes. "Oh, I already know what they're teaching," he told me. "In fact, I know more. But that's not the point.

"You see, after I retired, I found myself sitting around the house. I was pretty lonely. So I decided to enroll in this school. Now I come here to work on my own projects alongside the students. Sometimes, when a problem comes up, they turn to me. And sometimes, when I'm walking through the library and see these kids working on their designs, I just feel good. I'm part of their learning."

That's education as community.

But it doesn't do to idealize community colleges. Remember, "the only standard is variety." That's true of academic standards, as well. Today there's plenty of controversy over the quality of faculty and curriculum in America's two-year schools. Some of the critics focus on the nation's for-profit, "proprietary" schools (such as the truck driving schools I commented on in the section on transportation in Emerging Work). The most common complaints about these schools are that their graduates are so poorly trained that those who take out federal loans to finance their education fail to find work and are unable to repay them.

In many states, the proprietary schools are loosely regulated, so that quality varies; standards among the publicly funded community colleges may vary just as much. The main problem is keeping faculty current with rapidly-changing technology. While most community colleges don't guarantee lifetime employment through academic tenure, they nonetheless tend to employ the same teachers year after year.

Some schools have tried to meet this challenge by hiring mostly part-time instructors. One metro college, for example, has a full-time staff of five instructors and a part-time staff of three hundred. The argument for this arrangement is partly financial. Part-time staff are cheaper; they're paid by the course and don't receive benefits. (It's the same rationale the late Sam Walton followed in building his chain of Wal-Mart discount stores.)

The other argument is that the best way to keep faculty skills current is to hire practicing professionals with graduate degrees to teach part-time. For example, as new spreadsheet software is introduced to the field of accounting, a practicing accountant will be much more likely to learn the software and teach it to his students than will a full-time accounting professor who spends all his time teaching.

There's a lot to be said for this approach. But there are problems. Some question the amount of contact students have with faculty in a school full of moonlighting teachers. For one thing, during the past twenty years, the number of part-time students in the United States has doubled. Currently, 61 percent of students at public community colleges are enrolled part-time. Critics say that if both students and faculty are involved part-time, education suffers. There's likely to be no more contact than in a professional wrestling match or a discotheque.

They also point out that not all part-time instructors are professional people who turn to teaching just for the love of it. Many are underemployed teachers trying to survive, sometimes by teaching at four or five different institutions. A study by the American Association of University Professors found that 38 percent of part-time faculty members earn less than $20,000 a year. That's not a sign of successful professionals.

I've shared these data on part-time teachers to suggest the various levels of quality found in colleges today, and the need to be a careful consumer. There are, of course, many other factors one could consider, such as the quality of equipment and the library of a school.

In choosing a college and deciding whether to earn a credential, it's helpful to do some good information interviewing among people who are working in the field one is thinking of entering. Professional associations are a good resource. So are major employers in the field. That's where one can find out how professionals typically get their education, and where.

In addition, I often recommend asking a school for a referral to a recent graduate. While the school will undoubtedly pick one of its most successful grads (bypassing those alumni who are working on the grounds crew) one still can ask that graduate for referrals to a couple of others and get an idea of how students have viewed the place. It's Networking 101.

Another good strategy is to try to get work experience in the field one is studying while a student. That's especially important if one is entering a new field. Work experience not only enhances the learning process, it's also a good way to get employed.

The other day I met a woman who directs the newsroom at a large television station. She started there as an intern in a college program. Once at the station, she became so interested in the work going on there that she never completed her degree. That's not an uncommon story. Internships, like temporary employment services, provide a try-before-you-buy staging arena for both students and employers. It's not surprising that so many people begin their careers that way.

Volunteer assignments sometimes serve the same function. Many social service agencies offer an opportunity to learn certain skills, such as newsletter production, or to try working with particular populations, such as the elderly. Many colleges offer credit for the experience, sometimes under the heading of Cooperative Education. (See **Service-learning** under Resources.)

Most of all, whether or not one is pursuing a degree, I believe it's vitally important to find a learning place one enjoys. Last year I spent an exhilarating two weeks studying Spanish at a retreat center in the foothills outside Denver. The teachers were practitioners of "expanded learning," sometimes known as "accelerated learning"—a method of involving the whole person in the educational process. It was a remarkable experience. I've never had a dream in Spanish, after dabbling in the language for fifteen years. But several days into the course, I awoke with a headache at about 3:00 a.m. As I groped for the aspirin, suddenly I remembered my dream. I'd been trying to talk my way out of some crisis—in Spanish! No wonder my head hurt.

Two nights later I dreamt in Spanish again, but this time without a headache. Accelerated learning involves you like that. It's a deceptively powerful, childlike approach to education based on music and riddles and games. Eight hours a day, my classmates and I scrambled around like kids at recess, laughing and playing in Spanish. First, we'd learn a bit of vocabulary—say, parts of the body. Then we'd be given a skit or a contest to act out what we'd studied. The results were remarkable. For the first time, I found myself learning new words and phrases in order to communicate, not just to pass a test.

There was "espalda" (the Spanish word for "back"). One morning we read a play, espalda-a-espalda: back-to-back. "Feel the vibrations of your partner's breath through her back," our instructor said. I did, and remembered "espalda."

And "espada" ("sword"). I played a conquistador in one of our skits and had to learn what to call my sword.

Then there was "codo" ("elbow"). I broke into dance one day as we were singing a song, and caught another student in the eye with my elbow. Had I given her a black eye? Can they sue you for an "ojo negro?" I'll remember "codo."

That's accelerated learning. It's a process of weaving new information with all the facts and feelings of actual life, very much as children learn. As one of my teachers, Linda Moller, put it, "there are no memories without emotions."

Some believe that accelerated learning is three to five times faster than traditional language study. Diane Davalos, my other teacher, prefers the term "expanded learning." She says the point is not just to increase learning speed but to help the brain process information naturally, with the rest of the body.

I told her about dreaming in Spanish. "The brain loves that," she said. "We don't have to teach the brain how to think."

Indeed we don't, if we find our way to places where we can learn naturally. That begins when we remember that education is not a one-size-fits-all exercise, as it may have been back in school. It's a basic human function that combines the "holy curiosity of inquiry" with the benefits of staying current. Lifelong learning is living fully in our time. That's the gift of a changing economy.

Resources

The Learning Style Inventory by David Kolb, Personal Learning Guide, and related instruments are available from **McBER and Company**, 137 Newbury Street, Boston, Massachusetts 02116. Phone: (617) 437-7080.

The Institute for Certification of Computer Professionals is at 2200 East Devon Avenue, Suite 268, Des Plaines, Illinois 60018. Phone: (708) 299-4227.

The booklet *Lifelong Learning Trends* is available for $20.00 plus $3.00 postage and handling from the **National University Continuing Education Association**, Publications Office, One Dupont Circle, Suite 615, Washington, D.C. 20036-1168.

For an in-depth look at procedures for assessing prior learning, and a list of colleges with comprehensive assessment programs, see *Earn College Credit for What You Know* by Lois Lamdin. The book is available for $19.95 plus $4 shipping and handling from **The Council for Adult and Experiential Learning**, 223 West Jackson Boulevard, Suite 510, Chicago, Illinois 60606. Phone: (312) 922-5909.

The Society for Accelerated Learning and Teaching is at 3028 Emerson Avenue South, Minneapolis, Minnesota 55408. Phone: (800) 727-7620. *Accelerated Learning* by Colin Rose, a recommended book in the field, is available from SALT.

For information on **University of Phoenix** programs around the country, call (602) 966-9577. The central office is at 4615 East Elwood, P.O. Box 52069, Phoenix, Arizona 85072-2069.

The Status of Non-Tenure Track Faculty was published in November 1992 by **The American Association of University Profes-**

sors, 1012 Fourteenth Street, N.W., Suite 500, Washington, D.C. 20005. Phone: (202) 737-5900.

Service-learning: **The National Society for Internships and Experiential Education** publishes a *National Directory of Internships* with listings by geographical region and academic field. The book sells for $22. NSIEE is at 3509 Haworth Drive, Suite 207, Raleigh, North Carolina 27609.

The Cooperative Education Association is a related organization. They're at 3311 Toledo Terrace, Suite A101 #2, Hyattsville, Maryland 20782. Phone: (301) 559-8850.

The national office of **United Way** has created a computer system, Matchpoint, to keep tabs on skills and opportunities in volunteer assignments at member agencies. The system provides information on local agencies at more than 250 sites across the United States and Canada. For information on specific locations, call Pat Saccomandi at (800) 593-5654.

Spanish teacher Diane Davalos is at **Expanded Learning,** 125 West Second Avenue, Denver, Colorado 80223. Phone: (303) 722-2151.

Appendix

What Can You Do?

Jobs can be analyzed many ways—by salary, or technical specialty, or even whether one is "exempt" or "non-exempt" from overtime pay (that's a curious but traditional way to distinguish professional from staff positions).

It's more helpful to understand that all jobs consist of three basic elements: the *tasks* performed, the *skills* required, and the *traits* that enable us to work effectively. For example, an accountant prepares a tax return (*task*) using *skills* in tax law and accounting, knowledge of regulations that apply to the client's industry, and the ability to operate a particular computer software program. To do well in work of that kind, an individual needs certain *traits*: being detail-oriented and methodical.

A floral delivery driver delivers Mother's Day bouquets (task) using skills in driving, a knowledge of the city, and perhaps which flowers need to be delivered first before they wilt. To be most effective, the driver ought to have traits such as self-direction and friendliness.

We can perform a job analysis very simply by dividing a sheet of paper in thirds. We'll head the left-hand column "Task," the middle column "Skill," and the right-hand column "Trait." Here are examples of a job analysis of an accountant and floral delivery driver.

Accountant

Task	Skill	Trait
✦ prepare tax return	✦ knowledge of tax law and accounting	✦ detail-oriented
	✦ knowledge of regulations in client's industry	✦ methodical
	✦ ability to operate software program	

Floral Delivery Driver

Task	Skill	Trait
✦ deliver Mother's Day bouquets	✦ driving ability	✦ self-directed
	✦ knowledge of city	✦ courteous
	✦ knowledge of which flowers could wilt	

Now imagine that you are hiring someone as your replacement in your most recent job. Write down every task that the person would need to perform in the course of a week. When you've listed all the tasks, go back and fill in the skills. Then, do the same for two previous jobs.

Tasks: Duties a job requires.
Skills: Abilities required to perform the tasks.
Traits: Personal qualities to do the work effectively.

Task	Skill	Trait

Tasks: Duties a job requires.
Skills: Abilities required to perform the tasks.
Traits: Personal qualities to do the work effectively.

Task	Skill	Trait

Tasks: Duties a job requires.
Skills: Abilities required to perform the tasks.
Traits: Personal qualities to do the work effectively.

Task	Skill	Trait

Are there other jobs, family responsibilities, or volunteer roles where you develop skills that are important to you? Do a task/skill analysis of those experiences as well.

When you have finished your analysis, go back and draw a line through every task that you would prefer not to do again. Check every skill where you still seem to be growing.

Take a moment to look over your analysis and write down your reflections.

Notes: _____

_____

_____

_____

_____

Use the following worksheet to organize important skills from your task/skill/trait analysis. If your skills profile reminded you of other skills you've developed, write those down as well. Look for themes and patterns in the quadrants. When you find a cluster of skills, give it a title.

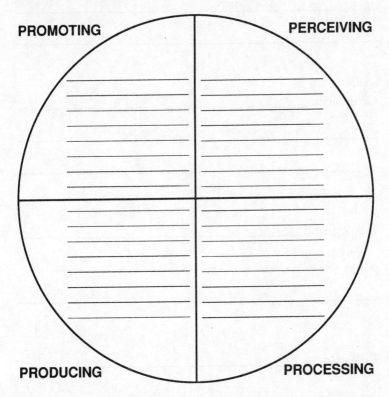

PROMOTING   **PERCEIVING**

PRODUCING   **PROCESSING**

Here is a worksheet to draft a resume. Begin with the "Capabilities" section, drawing on your worksheet data. If possible, find a partner for feedback. Don't be concerned about producing a perfect document. It's the process of trying to communicate our skills that counts.

Concentrate on your skills. Those are the basic branches of careers. Traits call for third-party endorsement; it's best to ask references to attest to our personal qualities.

Add your employment history, following the format of the sample resume: most recent job first. Then list your education the same way, and note your growing edges under "New Learning."

Resume Worksheet

Summary of qualifications: _____

_____

_____

Capabilities: _____

_____

_____

Employment: _____

_____

_____

Education: _____

_____

_____

New Learning: _____

_____

_____

You'll be in a better position to communicate with people from other industries, institutions, and occupations when you have a good grasp of your skills. Many of the people you approach may not understand very much about your job title or educational background, just as they wouldn't know how to perform the job you've done. But if you communicate in terms of *skills*, you're likely to find all sorts of connections among different occupations.

Index

About the Author

William Charland is an educational consultant and author of *The Heart of the Global Village*. He lives in Denver, Colorado. He writes from time to time on a variety of topics for *The Christian Science Monitor*.